BRITISH AUTHOR

Introductory Critical Studies

General Editor: ROBIN MAYHEAD

ALEXANDER POPE

In this Series

ALEXANDER POPE

BY

YASMINE GOONERATNE

Associate Professor of English
Macquarie University, New South Wales

CAMBRIDGE UNIVERSITY PRESS

CAMBRIDGE

LONDON · NEW YORK · MELBOURNE

Published by the Syndics of the Cambridge University Press
The Pitt Building, Trumpington Street, Cambridge CB2 1RP
Bentley House, 200 Euston Road, London NW1 2DB
32 East 57th Street, New York, NY 10022, USA
296 Beaconsfield Parade, Middle Park, Melbourne 3206, Australia

Library of Congress Cataloging in Publication Data

Gooneratne, Yasmine, 1935 –
Alexander Pope.

(British authors, introductory critical studies)
Includes index.
1. Pope, Alexander, 1688–1744 – Criticism and interpretation.
PR3634.G64   821'.5   76–4758
ISBN 0–521–21127–1
ISBN 0–521–29051–1 pbk.

First published 1976

Printed in Great Britain by
Western Printing Services Ltd
Bristol

For
BRENDON

General Preface

This study of Alexander Pope is the seventh in a series of short introductory critical studies of the more important British authors. The aim of the series is to go straight to the authors' works; to discuss them directly with a maximum of attention to concrete detail; to say what they are and what they do, and to indicate a valuation. The general critical attitude implied in the series is set out at some length in my *Understanding Literature*. Great literature is taken to be to a large extent self-explanatory to the reader who will attend carefully enough to what it says. 'Background' study, whether biographical or historical, is not the concern of the series.

It is hoped that this approach will suit a number of kinds of reader, in particular the general reader who would like an introduction which talks about the works themselves; and the student who would like a general critical study as a starting point, intending to go on to read more specialized works later. Since 'background' is not erected as an insuperable obstacle, readers in other English-speaking countries, countries where English is a second language, or even those for whom English is a foreign language, should find the books helpful. In Britain and the Commonwealth, students and teachers in universities and in the higher forms of secondary schools will find that the authors chosen for treatment are those most often prescribed for study in public and university examinations.

The series could be described as an attempt to make available to a wide public the results of the literary criticism of the last thirty years, and especially the methods associated with Cambridge. If the result is an increase in the reading, with enjoyment and understanding, of the great works of English literature, the books will have fulfilled their wider purpose.

ROBIN MAYHEAD

Note

All quotations are taken from the following edition of the Twickenham Text, in one volume with selected annotations: *The Poems of Alexander Pope*, ed. John Butt (London, Methuen, first published 1963; 2nd ed. used here, 1965).

Contents

ix

Introductory

A.   Be sure *your self* and your own *Reach* to know,   48
            How far your *Genius, Taste,* and *Learning* go;
            Launch not beyond your Depth, but be discreet,
            And mark *that Point* where Sense and Dulness *meet.*
                Nature in all things fix'd the Limits fit,
            And wisely curb'd proud Man's pretending Wit . . .

              A perfect Judge will *read* each Work of Wit   233
            With the same Spirit that its Author *writ,*
            Survey the *Whole,* nor seek slight Faults to find,
            Where *Nature moves,* and *Rapture warms* the Mind;
            Nor lose, for that malignant dull Delight,
            The *gen'rous Pleasure* to be charm'd with Wit . . .
            In Wit, as Nature, what affects our Hearts   243
            Is not th'Exactness of peculiar Parts;
            'Tis not a *Lip,* or *Eye,* we Beauty call,
            But the joint Force and full *Result of all.*
            Thus when we view some well-proportion'd Dome,
            (The *World's* just Wonder, and ev'n *thine O Rome!*)
            No single Parts unequally surprize;
            All comes *united* to th'admiring Eyes;
            No monstrous Height, or Breadth, or Length appear;
            The *Whole* at once is *Bold,* and *Regular.*
                   From *An Essay on Criticism* (1711)

This passage from Pope's poetry embodies some of the central paradoxes of his work. A modern reader would sense at once that there is energy and richness here, but that present-day usage of terms such as 'Nature', 'Wit', 'Genius', 'Taste' and 'Sense' prevents him from fully appreciating them. The confident authority with which Pope refers to these terms as if they were permanent points of reference, touchstones that must outlast time and change, was possible only in an age of political and cultural stability. Pope shared with other cultivated Englishmen of the early eighteenth century a sense of being 'Augustans', living in an enlightened age in which literature had reached the highest point of purity and refinement. His best poetry expresses the living values of that age, and demonstrates how a good writer can simultaneously speak to and for his society: representing those values, he can at the same time extend and criticise them.

Dictionary definitions help us to understand those values better than current usage can. 'Genius', for instance, which we would interpret as an extraordinary capacity for imaginative creation, meant for Pope and his contemporaries a natural ability or quality of mind. 'Taste', which for us would be probably limited to the way we dress ourselves or furnish our houses, ranged much more widely for Pope, who used it to signify the faculty of perceiving and enjoying excellence in art, literature and the like. 'Sense' meant natural understanding and intelligence, practical soundness of judgment. But the two words that recur throughout Pope's work are 'Nature' and 'Wit'. We see from the definition supplied above that both 'Genius' and 'Sense' were regarded as *natural*; like a good many of the philosophical and critical terms Pope uses, these words derive their meanings from the Augustan view of 'Nature' as the inherent dominating power or impulse by which action or character is determined, directed or controlled. Here, as often in eighteenth-century poetry, 'Nature' is personified: as a kindly but strict goddess, who places 'curbs' upon ambitious critics, she provides the moving force behind great literature (line 236). The later, more familiar use of the word 'Nature' to include the features and products of the earth itself as contrasted with those of human civilisation, does not operate in poetry until the Romantic period. For Pope 'Nature' was still an all-inclusive term, covering the impulses of man and animals, plants and winds, streams and planets alike, the diversity of which filled him with a sense of wonder at the magnitude of the power that could order and control them all. To a poet who sees 'Nature' at work in every part of the world around him, a gentleman discussing politics and literature in a London coffee-house is as 'natural' to his proper environment as a hunter fitting an arrow to his bow must be in a forest.

'Wit', originally meaning 'the mind', has many extensions, most of which were in operation at the time Pope wrote. The word could mean the faculty of thinking and reasoning in general, or practical talent, skill or ingenuity. In the seventeenth century 'Wit' went further than cleverness, to include that quality of speech or writing which consists in the apt association of thoughts or expressions calculated to surprise or delight by their unexpectedness. A 'wit' was a person of superior mental capacity; possessed of judgment and discretion, he had a talent for saying brilliant (and true) things in a sparkling way, and a lively fancy that made his conversation a delight to his friends and associates. Opposed to 'Wit' is 'Dulness', and the critic who cannot appreciate works of true 'wit' is appropriately 'malignant' and 'dull'. It is an antipathy we recall when we read Pope's *Dunciad*, and find a literary 'world' divided between the forces of Wit and light and those of Dulness, darkness and evil.

A good many of Pope's words have lost levels of meaning in coming down to us: 'admiring', for instance, once conveyed more than appreciation, it involved sensations of stunned surprise leading to profound, even awe-struck pleasure. The true critic's heartfelt approval was won, therefore, by 'well-proportion'd' work that reflected 'Nature', the 'natural' order of a harmonious universe, and – an appropriate simile for an English Augustan writing in the period when St Paul's Cathedral both represented and influenced current ideals of architectural dignity and beauty – the 'regulated boldness' of Palladian architecture (lines 247–52).

Let us look at some other examples of Pope's poetry:

B. Oft when the World imagine Women stray,   91
The *Sylphs* thro' mystick Mazes guide their Way,
Thro' all the giddy Circle they pursue,
And old Impertinence expel by new.
What tender Maid but must a Victim fall
To one Man's Treat, but for another's Ball?
When *Florio* speaks, what Virgin could withstand,
If gentle *Damon* did not squeeze her Hand?
With varying Vanities, from ev'ry Part,
They shift the moving Toyshop of their Heart;
Where Wigs with Wigs, with Sword-knots Sword-knots
        strive,
Beaus banish Beaus, and Coaches Coaches drive.
                    From *The Rape of the Lock*, 1 (1714)

C.   – On superior pow'rs   241
Were we to press, inferior might on ours:
Or in the full creation leave a void,
Where, one step broken, the great scale's destroy'd:
From Nature's chain whatever link you strike,
Tenth or ten thousandth, breaks the chain alike.
    And if each system in gradation roll,
Alike essential to th'amazing whole;

The least confusion but in one, not all
That system only, but the whole must fall.
Let Earth unbalanc'd from her orbit fly,   251
Planets and Suns run lawless thro' the sky,
Let ruling Angels from their spheres be hurl'd,
Being on being wreck'd, and world on world,
Heav'n's whole foundations to their centre nod,
And Nature tremble to the throne of God:
All this dread ORDER break – for whom? for thee?
Vile worm! – oh Madness, Pride, Impiety!

> From *An Essay on Man*, I (1734)

D.   'Odious! in woollen! 'twould a Saint provoke,   242
(Were the last words that poor Narcissa spoke)
No, let a charming Chintz, and Brussels lace
Wrap my cold limbs, and shade my lifeless face:
One would not, sure, be frightful when one's dead –
And – Betty – give this Cheek a little Red.'

> From *An Epistle to Lord Cobham* (1734)

Taken together, passages A, B, C and D present a view of the world and man's place in it very different from present-day ideas. Passage A, advising writers to *limit* and *curb* their ambitions, stresses caution to a degree that must irritate those who believe literary expression must be 'free' and unfettered by rules if it is to convey personal opinion and experience naturally and spontaneously. Pope's view of the carping critic as a 'malignant' growth on literature would seem an exaggeration to a reader who does not share the Augustan view of literature as an expression of universal, 'natural' order. The ironic thanks in passage B that society beauties are preserved by their own frivolity for the respectability of marriage might seem pointless now, when marriage itself has been called in question. Can we claim with Pope's confidence in passage C that there is a creator-God at the centre of our universe? And the satire on feminine vanity carried to death's very door might seem irrelevant in an age when morticians are almost indistinguishable from beauticians, and the use of cosmetics is no longer reserved for ladies of fashion or the actress who was the model for Pope's 'Narcissa'. Finally, the medium of all four passages is the rhymed 'heroic' couplet, completely at odds with present literary practice except in the hands of the occasional academic poet who uses it for special purposes. Can the modern reader find anything to interest him here? The themes of Pope's poetry seem to refer to a vanished past and to values long dead and forgotten; can they interest any beside academics and antiquarians?

If the passages are read again, this time as poetry and not merely for their subject matter, probably the first thing to secure our attention would be the passionate engagement of the poet's emotion in passage C. This begins in an orderly, reasoned manner like that used to expound literary criteria in A. But at about line 251 – as the sense that the great system of natural order he has described is in danger of destruction enters the poet's consciousness – the poem seems to take wings, rising rhythmically upon one destructive image after another until a climax is reached in line 256 –

> And Nature tremble to the throne of God.

If we turn now to the passage from Book IV of *The Dunciad* quoted in Chapter 9, pages 145–6, we see that the remarkable energy generated in each passage derives from the same source, a vision of an all-pervading world order, and horror at the thought of its destruction. Since we write with greatest sincerity and skill about what interests or moves us deeply, since we know from our reading that writers become vague when they write about things that concern them only in an abstract and general way, is not the texture of the verse in passage C (a piece of verse that describes an abstract system of values) surprising in its power to make us visualise, hear and feel what is being described? The heightened imagination that produces the caving-in image of collapse in

> Heav'n's whole foundations to their centre nod

and masterly management of rhythm that effects the transition of mood in the last two lines – what are we to make of these? One can understand a dedicated poet getting angry, eloquent, even prophetic about the collapse of literary values, but what is one to think of a poet who writes with such feeling and technical mastery about a system of abstract philosophy?

The movement of Pope's verse, its verbal exactness and precise imagery are the most dependable proofs that he was intensely moved, imaginatively and emotionally, by neo-classical ideas about the universe current in his age, and that he turned them into something of his own. From the energy generated by his passionate grasp of these ideas (see Chapter 7, in which his expression of them in *An Essay on Man* is considered) spring the currents that connect the main source of power with other aspects of his experience as man and poet. Abstract as the rules set out in passage A are, we can see that the ideas behind them harmonise with the general scheme of the universe described in passage C. Passages B and D achieve their ironic effect because a code of values is implicit in each. By all the rules of reason and order, the behaviour of the 'tender maids' and of 'Narcissa' lack decorum. A woman's heart was not meant to be a 'moving Toyshop' – that it has become one is an offence against Nature, *human* nature as well as the more universal sense Pope generally has in mind when he uses the word. 'Poor' Narcissa's vanity is, similarly, an offence against Nature, deserving no pity from the poet nor sentimental tears from the reader.

Pope's poetry draws its raw materials from life in his time. We could compile a fairly comprehensive picture of social and literary life in eighteenth-century England from the details in his poems. He is his age's most representative writer, so much at ease in the literary modes of his time that he was compelled to sacrifice neither personal nor artistic integrity in order to write. It was an age of rules, of accepted genres in life as well as in art and literature, and Pope reaches in his work the heights of skill and significance possible to those who work within such accepted contemporary limits. As we have seen, he wrote passionately-felt poetry in exposition and defence of the moral and artistic values that guided him and other cultivated men of his time. Order was for him an ideal, an organising principle that amounted to a moral necessity, and he saw Wit, Sense, Taste, Reason and Decorum as the means by which that morally-directed Order maintained its proper control of human values and behaviour.

If we examine passages A to D again, referring this time to the poems from which they are taken, we discover that, personal as some of them seem and revelatory as they are of Pope's approach to his own poetry, they are all what we call 'genre' pieces. Passages A and C are from 'essays', versified treatises intended to instruct and/or debate. Passage D is an 'imitation' (a transformation into English contemporary idiom) of the work of the Latin poet Horace. Passage B is from a poem in the genre of the 'mock-heroic', deliberately modelled in structure and aspects of its technique on Homer's epic poem, *The Iliad*, and relying for its fullest effect upon the reader's familiarity with the original. So they are all 'public' poems, belonging to established forms or patterns recognisable by Pope's contemporaries, and gaining in value by being so recognised.

Pope's concept of 'originality' was therefore not ours. 'Epistles', 'Essays', 'Imitations', 'Satires', 'Epic Poems' – these were well-defined kinds of poetic expression, each with a set of rules. The poet's 'originality' had to work within those rules, his invention bending them to his own purposes. To Pope the rules derived from ancient poetic practice were not as restricting as they came to seem to later writers. To him the rules were 'useful', indeed – as we see in passage A – even 'natural'. As aids to writing well, the rules set out in *An Essay on Criticism* (see Chapter 2) provided a useful framework, but were not necessarily an end in themselves. Pope shows himself careful to abide by them in his apprentice work (see the discussion of his *Pastorals* in Chapter 2) but he recognised early that the gifted writer could and must 'snatch a Grace beyond the Reach of Art'. It is not that a great writer could ignore the rules, but that a Shakespeare, a Milton, a Dryden – or a Pope – wins through to this 'Grace' by reaching *in the same direction* as the less gifted observers of the rules, until he is carried by his 'genius' across the level of mere adherence to which their limited talents restrict them, into the realm where genius, expressing itself, expresses also that 'Nature' on which the rules are based.

Pope's meticulous adherence to generic rules when writing the most personal of poetry gives some modern readers the puzzling impression that he projects quite different personalities in successive poems. In his *Essay on Man* (1730), for example, he seems to adopt the posture of moralist and teacher. The *Epistle to Dr Arbuthnot*, however, written only a year later, contains a portrait of a contemporary as a double-tongued, abnormal oddity –

> His Wit all see-saw between *that* and *this*, 323
> Now high, now low, now Master up, now Miss,
> And he himself one vile Antithesis.

Two years after creating this clever caricature, in 1733, Pope says in the *Imitation of the First Satire of the Second Book of Horace* that his dearest wish is to expose himself to the judgment of his age as frankly and openly as he judges his own friends and enemies. How is the reader to reconcile these 'personalities' which seem to cancel out one another? If there is a 'real' Pope in one of these poetic personalities, what are we to say of the others? There is a further problem: on occasion – especially in Pope's maturest work, such as the *Epistle to Dr Arbuthnot* and the *Imitations of Horace* – these differing 'personalities' speak successively in the same poem.

The different 'faces' or 'voices' of Pope have been described by scholars and critics as *personae*, masks that separate the audience/reader from the real person who wears and manipulates them. But *personae* is a term associated with acting, and with the special device used by writers to project a certain kind of personality into a fictional world (a good example is Swift's use of his character, Lemuel Gulliver, in *Gulliver's Travels*). The word carries overtones of pretence, falsehood and ambiguity that should not be linked with the work of a dedicated *poet* of the kind Pope often declared himself to be. A writer of fiction or a dramatist necessarily works behind the scenes; his purposes must be achieved indirectly, through skilful manipulation of his characters. The poet's procedure is different, being more open and direct in its expression of a personal point of view. Part of his integrity must depend on his power to express with greater and greater intensity of truth, feeling and perception, his sense of life. His growth as a poet depends on the single-mindedness and success with which he strives for such true expression. And pretence and falsehood have nothing to do with this kind of effort.

> I love to pour out all myself, as plain   51
> As downright *Shippen*, or as old *Montagne*.
> In them, as certain to be lov'd as seen,
> The Soul stood forth, nor kept a Thought within;
> In me what Spots (for Spots I have) appear
> Will prove at least the Medium must be clear.
> In this impartial Glass, my Muse intends
> Fair to expose myself, my Foes, my Friends;
> Publish the present Age, but where my Text
> Is Vice too high, reserve it for the next . . .

So wrote Pope in his *Imitation of the First Satire of the Second Book of Horace*. The 'impartial Glass' into which wine is to be poured is like the 'medium' through which the truth about the poet and his society will be revealed. The parallel shows how aware Pope was that in poetry the truth about a writer must always appear, whether consciously or not. The image he uses is of a clear crystal goblet of old wine: the wine of this poet's personality is both mature and unadulterated, in the connoisseur's sense of the words 'old' and 'downright'. The glass is held up to the light, and turned slowly in the hand of an appreciative and well-judging gentleman, a true 'Augustan'. The idea bears some relationship to that other image in which Dryden somewhat patronisingly referred to the poetry of a great predecessor: 'Chaucer, I confess, is a rough diamond, and must be polish'd ere he shines.' Pope followed Dryden's example in 'polishing' Chaucer to the requirements of refined eighteenth-century tastes (see Chapter 2). To shine, to give off and reflect light (which is, in both contexts, synonymous with 'Truth') is the true function of the poet. And what Pope did, or thought he was doing, for Chaucer, life itself did for Pope.

The mention of Dryden in connection with Pope's poetry – and especially in connection with its essential 'truth' – should lead us back in time to their literary ancestor, Milton. Pope and Milton wrote very different 'kinds' of poetry, but they agreed in their notion of the poet's calling as a heaven-directed one, with Truth as its goal. Preparing themselves for a future as great poets was not only a matter of collecting, studying and practising technical skills, but also of developing the kind of personality that would reflect and transmit the truth about life and be itself clear enough of serious flaws to be able to do so. Milton reflected ironically in *Lycidas* that he had kept himself from the degenerating influences of courtly amatory poetry, only to find his own high aims clouded over with doubts and fears at the news of the untimely death of his friend and fellow-poet, Edward King. This is matched by Pope's equally ironic inclusion of the poet's ceaseless pursuit of his Muse in a list of misguided human activities in the *Essay on Man* (II, 261–70). At times both poets met with doubts and discouragements, but both recovered. And Pope, who inherited Milton's poetic legacy through Dryden, strengthened it into an active tradition that passes after his death to George Crabbe and Byron. Pope's poetry is therefore a very important literary meeting-point, as well as the expression of individual genius. And although there is another, minor, poetic tradition that comes from Spenser and the minor Milton, to be carried on by Gray and Collins through Keats to Tennyson, the greatest strain of English poetry is that to which Pope belongs, and which he does so much to strengthen and enrich.

In its integrity as much as in its technical virtuosity, Pope's poetry reveals him to be Milton's heir. The impression that its variety reflects a chameleon-like personality resolves into a truer picture when the poetry is read chronologically. Over years of constant writing, the poems present a matchless record of what happens when experiences of varying intensity strike upon a poet's imagination as revelatory truth. The impact of experience, registered and recorded ('reflected'), resembles the chipping of a diamond and its subsequent polishing to reveal a facet, that facet adding its own brilliance to the results of other successive impacts of fresh experience. So the bewildering variety of poetic 'personalities' resolve themselves into the complex personality of a great poet developing over forty years of continuous authorship.

For this reason a chronological approach to Pope's poetry is useful, and is followed in this book. Each of the poems considered in the following chapters can stand by itself: it is the authentic expression of a poet's total personality at a particular period. But all – and especially the later poems – gain if we have previous acquaintance with the verses Pope made earlier. Even the most finished of his poems is so intimately related to the original experience that, reading it, we re-live the experience with him. And it is worth remembering that the *writing* of a poem was for Pope an experience too; we shall examine later several poems where the doubts, uncertainties, near-failures and ultimate triumphs in the *writing* are recorded as faithfully as the original experience. Our response to the brilliantly coruscating personality and the assured technical skills revealed in the *Epistle to Dr Arbuthnot* will be more valuable if we have watched Pope battle for his psychological and artistic balance in writing the *Elegy to the Memory of an Unfortunate Lady*, and appreciated the deliberateness with which those technical skills were sought and exercised in apprentice work like the *Pastorals*, and even *The Rape of the Lock*. To read his poems in the chronological order of their publication is to become witnesses to the process by which a great poet is made. This is possible for us because of the intensity with which Pope dedicated himself to Poetry, and therefore to Truth.

The images of light and energy that come naturally to the mind when reading Pope's poetry are, I suggest, more appropriate media for approaching his work than the limited (and rather dubious) *personae* of fiction and dramatic illusion. When Pope resorts to 'pretence', he does so deliberately, making his intention clear: in writing the *Pastorals* he adopts a rural scene and manner to suit the literary mode he happens to be experimenting with. It is a temporary measure, for he tells us that he will leave the pastoral mode (as Milton did before him) for other kinds of writing when the time is right. In one sense, however – and I think in that sense only – the 'personalities' Pope projects are real masks, with the same function as the changing colours with which certain living creatures imitate their background, so escaping the predator's eye. In certain obvious and painful ways, Pope was isolated from his background, handicapped and vulnerable. In a society ruled by powerful upper-class Protestants, he was the son of a Roman Catholic linen-draper. Among gentlemen whose pursuits and style of dress emphasised manliness and vigour, Pope's small size and sickly figure attracted immediate (and often contemptuous or pitying) notice. Driven by his idea of a future as a great English poet, Pope had to bear the in-dignity of being puny and deformed. The need to conform and identify with his background must have been strong for him, just as it was for Jane Austen, an observant ironist living an apparently placid life in a village of mediocrities. And so, though Pope's acceptance of the eighteenth-century world-view as it came to him through Bolingbroke and his expression of it in *An Essay on Man* are backed by strong personal convictions of his own, the poem is coloured by a desire to produce what would be generally acceptable. Pope's talent was acknowledged early by the critics, and his reputation as a poet grew quickly. But that talent and fame attracted jealous enemies, whose personal attacks had to be countered without loss of dignity. Pope's entry upon the form of satiric poetry, his discovery that his poetic powers were exactly suited to it, must have seemed a God-given way out of a psychological morass:

> Yes, I am proud; I must be proud to see   208
> Men not afraid of God, afraid of me:
> Safe from the Bar, the Pulpit, and the Throne,
> Yet touch'd and sham'd by *Ridicule* alone.

> O sacred Weapon! left for Truth's defence,
> Sole Dread of Folly, Vice, and Insolence!
> To all but Heav'n-directed hands deny'd,
> The Muse may give thee, but the Gods must guide.
> Rev'rent I touch thee!
>
> From *Epilogue to the Satires*, II (1738)

In satire Pope could moralise with religious fervour, he could be seen in wit and intellectual and moral power to tower over his contemporaries as he could not in the street, the salon or the coffee-house. Best of all, his poetic skill had become so great that he could take on all-comers in a way denied him in physical combat. If we can understand this poet's dilemma as a member of a handicapped minority in a strong, confused, yet in many ways admirable society, we go far towards understanding why poetry meant so much to him. It was Pope's life. It was also his means of coping with life. And because it was touched and modified by so many important features of the contemporary milieu, Pope's poetry reflects his era.

A second aspect of Pope's poetry that confuses some modern readers is partly a result of his representativeness: his frequent use of allusion. In poems such as the Horatian *Epistles* and *Satires*, and particularly in *The Dunciad*, the reader meets scores of contemporary names, some now forgotten. Some of these people are given their full names, some (prudently) disguised by the use of consonants and asterisks, and some by a fairly transparent pseudonym, such as 'Atticus' for the poet/critic Joseph Addison, and 'Sporus' and 'Sappho' for Pope's enemies, Lord William Hervey and Lady Mary Wortley Montagu. Where the allusion can still be grasped, the reference takes on added meaning: as in the 'Roman' flavour of the name 'Atticus', which subtly enhances the moral indignation behind Pope's assertion that Addison had debased the Roman ideals of just and judicious literary criticism. But often the link is lost, and the allusions remain as a string of unfamiliar names. The only way to deal with these is to make use of a reliable editor's footnotes. In a sense Pope's comment that *The Dunciad* was not made for the people it refers to, but the people for the poem, is confirmed by the reader's own experience. So vividly is a context and a situation created – as in the sewer games in Book II of *The Dunciad* – that we grasp what Pope wishes to convey about the personages involved (in this case the *literary* ineptitude and *moral* slovenliness of the writers who are depicted by him as physically rolling and plunging in depths of mud, slush and excrement) without any real need of a more particular knowledge of their names and reputations.

The personal element in Pope's satiric poetry has in any case been exaggerated: who were 'Narcissa'? 'Atossa'? 'Cloe'? Does it matter? Pope has transcended the originals, so that what began as caricature ends as a satiric portrait of a human type. 'Narcissa' symbolises vanity, just as 'Atticus' symbolises a literary arrogance that defeats its own purposes. 'Nature does nothing in vain', wrote Pope in 1712, in a letter to the *Spectator* (No. 404, Friday, 13 June 1712):

the Creator of the Universe has appointed every thing to a certain Use and Purpose, and determined it to a settled Course and Sphere of Action, from which, if it in the least deviates, it becomes unfit to answer those Ends for which it was designed. In like Manner is it in the Dispositions of Society . . . It is, I think, pretty plain, that most of the Absurdity and Redicule [*sic*] we meet with in the World, is generally owing to the impertinent Affectation of excelling in Characters Men are not fit for, and for which Nature never designed them . . . For my Part, I could never consider this preposterous Repugnancy to Nature any otherwise, than not only as the greatest Folly, but also one of the most heinous Crimes, since it is a direct Opposition to the Disposition of Providence, and, (as *Tully* expresses it) like the Sin of the Giants, an actual Rebellion against Heaven.

In the parallel with Titanic folly here we find a clue to the urgency and passion latent in Pope's satiric portraits. For all their grace and charm, Belinda of *The Rape of the Lock* and Narcissa of the *Epistle to Lord Cobham* are rebels against the 'settled Course' and fundamental laws of order and reason expounded in *An Essay on Man*; their unruliness must be checked by the power of the 'sacred Weapon', satire.

A different type of allusiveness may be seen in the characters from Greek myth, classical criticism, and epic poetry that people Pope's verse. Modern readers without a formal education in the Greek and Roman classics find that they cannot understand parts of Pope's poetry without a classical dictionary. It is worth keeping in mind that the world of Greek myth and legend was familiar to an eighteenth-century English poet, and its characters, human and divine, are only half-jocularly employed for decorative and rhetorical effects. There is a sense in which the hidden power of the old myths reasserts itself in eighteenth-century poetry, and no writer of the period was more responsive to that power than Pope. The long-term exposure to Greek poetry involved in Pope's translation of *The Iliad* makes Homer and the Muses seem as engagingly alive in his poetry as the frequenters of Button's coffee-house:

> Ye sacred Nine! that all my Soul possess,   259
> Whose Raptures fire me, and whose Visions bless,
> Bear me, oh bear me to sequester'd Scenes,
> The Bow'ry Mazes and surrounding Greens;
> To *Thames*'s Banks which fragrant Breezes fill,
> Or where ye Muses sport on *Cooper*'s Hill.
> From *Windsor Forest* (1713)

Poets do not today invoke the Muses, the daughters of Memory and patron deities of the Greek arts. They do not invite their inspiration in the writing of a poem. That is not to say that poets no longer sense the movement within themselves of powers not merely rational or conscious: but that in an age of unbelief, the poet hesitates to attribute that power to a divine origin. For Pope, however, although he was writing in the eighteenth century and in England, as a Roman Catholic in a society dominated by Christian values, the Greek Muses were still very much alive. His invocation of their 'sacred' power is no mere rhetorical figure: *Windsor Forest* lives as a poem because of their kindly activity in consenting to grace and bless a particular spot of English rural ground, and in doing so to sanction the continuation of the classical tradition in English poetry. In this poem the 'Sicilian Muses' of Theocritus and 'Mantuan Nymphs' of Virgil arrive when appropriately invoked by an English poet, to give the banks of the Thames a pastoral air, to stray in the 'groves of academe' at Oxford and Cambridge, to assist in the composition of a shepherds' duet, and to create the correct atmosphere for an elegy.

Such a recognition of the Muses' power over the dedicated artist as Pope evinces throughout his work, came about through his assimilation of Greek and Latin literature, and his ability to achieve a synthesis between his Christian inheritance and a classical, essentially 'pagan' tradition. Such a synthesis had been made before by other poets, chief among whom was Milton. But Pope re-makes it, in personal terms that tell us a great deal about his

relationship with his craft, creating in the shadow of the
mysterious and 'sacred Nine' his own humbler Muse, a personal
deity who guards and symbolises his own poetry:

> O let my Muse her slender Reed inspire,   11
> 'Till in your Native Shades You tune the Lyre:
> So when the Nightingale to Rest removes,
> The Thrush may chant to the forsaken Groves,
> But, charm'd to Silence, listens while She sings,
> And all th'Aerial Audience clap their Wings.
>
> From *Spring* (1704)

In these lines, dedicated to his mentor, Sir William Trumbull,
Pope assigns to his Muse the position appropriate to a beginning
talent: she plays the homely 'thrush' to Sir William's 'night-
ingale'. There is an additional, melancholy strain in the short
Hymn Written in Windsor Forest (1717) where the young poet
accepts his Muse from the 'sacred Nine' as compensation for
worldly satisfactions he will have to do without –

> All hail! once pleasing, once inspiring Shade,
>   Scene of my youthful Loves, and happier hours!
> Where the kind Muses met me as I stray'd,
>   And gently press'd my hand, and said, Be Ours! –
> Take all thou e'er shalt have, a constant Muse:
>   At Court thou may'st be lik'd, but nothing gain;
> Stocks thou may'st buy and sell, but always lose;
>   And love the brightest eyes, but love in vain!

This belief in the 'constancy' or faithfulness of his Muse (here
contrasted wryly with fickle fortune and human affections) is
repeated much more strongly in the last lines of the *Elegy to the
Memory of an Unfortunate Lady*, in which the Muse shares with
the 'Lady' of the poem (who has come in the course of it to
symbolise generous and sympathetic affection) the last thought of
the dying poet (lines 75–82).

As Pope matured, his relationship with his art and its presiding
deity seems to have become increasingly personal and complex.
Ironic allusions to the Muse are frequent in the years that saw
Pope engaged in literary warfare (connected with his translation
of Homer's *Iliad* in an atmosphere of envy and rivalry); editing
Shakespeare, and seeing his work unfairly (as he thought) criticised; and producing in his first version of *The Dunciad* a satire
on literary society so biting that it was not clear to his contemporaries where malice ended in it and morality began. Describing

the products of the Temple of Dulness in *The Dunciad* (1728) as

> the Fool's paradise, the Statesman's scheme, 9
> The air-built Castle, and the golden Dream,
> The Maid's romantic wish, the Chymist's flame,

Pope ironically adds his own poetic ambition to the list of classic impossibilities –

> And Poet's vision of eternal fame. 12

Two years later Pope equates the dedicated poet with the alchemist tied to his experiments by the delusion that he will succeed one day in making gold:

> Whate'er the Passion, knowledge, fame, or pelf 261
> Not one will change his neighbour with himself,
> The learn'd is happy nature to explore,
> The fool is happy that he knows no more;
> The rich is happy in the plenty giv'n,
> The poor contents him with the care of Heav'n.
> See the blind beggar dance, the cripple sing.
> The sot a hero, lunatic a king;
> The starving chemist in his golden views
> Supremely blest, the poet in his muse.
>
> From *An Essay on Man* (1734)

Lines 261–6 seem straightforward, but the next four pile irony upon irony, causing us to reflect on possible ambiguities earlier; and the *poet*, arriving at the end of the passage, is at once its climactic point (the individual least likely to wish his condition changed) and the comprehensive symbol of every listed foolishness, carrying in himself the qualities of scholar and idiot, rich man and beggar. Blind, crippled, drunken, mad, misguided, besotted, he is content with a wretched condition: the poet's life. No doubt this passage was written with one eye on the Grub Street hack starving in his garret, but the other dwells ironically on Pope's own passionate attachment to his craft, his perpetual pursuit of his divine mistress. In the *Epistle to Dr Arbuthnot* (1735) ironic reflections on the poet's vocation recur:

> Why did I write? what sin to me unknown 125
> Dipt me in Ink, my Parents', or my own?

A cynical note, originating in the lines immediately preceding these, sheds a gloomy complexity on the caricature of Christian baptism with which Pope symbolises a literary initiation. In one sense the act of writing is a washing away of original sin, but in another the dipping in black ink suggests that his unsuspecting and eager adoption of a writer's life was a subtle form of divine punishment. Pope had already shown in his *Dunciad* (1728) that the literary life involved a good deal of dirt- and mud-slinging, slander, and character-blackening. By taking upon himself this difficult burden he might be expiating earlier unknown sins. Yet, as the paragraph develops and Pope continues to contemplate his life's work (and spiritual self-dedication is implicit in the image of baptism), the feeling of the poem shifts and alters. Bitterness and cynicism subside, and soothing ideas of poetry as a healing, restorative influence prevail. It is a good instance of the way wit can expose and emphasise a tragic or despairing moment, yet simultaneously exorcise the self-pity such exposure invites –

> The Muse but serv'd to ease some Friend, not Wife,   131
> To help me thro' this long Disease, my Life,
> To second, ARBUTHNOT! thy Art and Care,
> And teach, the Being you preserv'd, to bear.

The wit – a combination of feeling, intelligence, and long practice in the art of sparkling, epigrammatic expression – that helps Pope to make a joke of his disability is of the kind we call 'metaphysical' in the poetry of Donne or Herbert. The vision of the Muse as sickroom attendant startles us, and yet on closer consideration we see that the homely metaphor is very apt: it awakens a sense of the long-standing relationship between the poet and his art, suggesting how it has come to include affection, gratitude, patience, constancy. It establishes itself through the alliteration that marries 'long' with 'Life', to reinforce the impression of prolonged suffering derived from the word 'Disease'. Later in the same poem Pope reflects on the abuse Grub Street has lavished on his poetry, parentage, religion and physical deformity (lines 378–81). Pope rarely refers to the last: we infer from this silence, how much his ability to project a powerful self-image in his poetry must have compensated for his physical limitations. When he does make a direct reference, he does not dwell on his condition with self-pity, but includes it in a catalogue which indicates to the reader how intensely he suffered from his weaknesses, and the attacks upon them. The Muse has now a personality and a history for her poet: she has been faithful to him, eased his sickness, comforted him, and borne insult for his sake. She is a part of him.

When Pope decided to become a satiric poet in the Horatian

manner, the Muse turns a new facet to the light. Imbued with
moral purpose, she becomes the spirit of Truth. The *Epistles* and
Satires exercise to the full Pope's observant eye for contemporary
weaknesses. They draw his talent for satire, his skill with the
caustic allusion, the unanswerable line, to the service of moral
reform. But they offer no scope for wandering in the maze of
'fancy' or the imagination. In turning to satire Pope deliberately
put fanciful poetry behind him, and it is clear from the tone of
the relevant passage in his *Epistle to Dr Arbuthnot* (lines 334–41)
that he saw this step as a necessary one in his long pilgrimage
towards the writing of great poetry, the verse in which he would
strive to 'match the Bards whom none e'er match'd before'.[1] That

---

[1] *Imitations of Horace*, Book II, Epistle II (1737), line 115. It has been
suggested that there is a link between Pope's deliberate adoption of elevated subject matter for the poetry he wrote after 1731 and his expansion and ornamentation of the subterranean grotto between his house and
his garden at Twickenham in the years between 1731 and 1740; as if 'his
native impulse toward the feigned and extravagant, diverted from
expression in his writing, now . . . turned to his gardens and grotto' (F.
Bracher, 'Pope's Grotto: The Maze of Fancy' (1949), reprinted in May-
nard Mack (ed.), *Essential Articles for the Study of Pope* (1964), pp. 97–
121). The essential elements of a grotto are overhanging rock, running
water, moss, trailing vines and shining minerals, and go back to the
classical *nymphaeum*, a natural cave with a spring, supposedly the home
of a nymph. The poetic tradition by which grottoes and caves were
regarded as a haunt of the Muses was echoed in the seventeenth and
eighteenth centuries by Milton, Thomas Warton and others. Pope
expanded his natural cavern into halls or chambers, in which he engaged
with his friends in literary and philosophical discussion; and it seems
evident, from his *Verses on a Grotto . . . at Twickenham* (1741) that he
had begun to construct a personal myth of his own around the grotto and
the Muses who resided there:

> Lo th'Aegerian Grott,
> Where, nobly-pensive, ST JOHN sate and thought;
> Where *British* sighs from dying WYNDHAM stole,
> And the bright Flame was shot thro' MARCHMONT's Soul.
> Let such, such only, tread this sacred Floor,
> Who dare to love their Country, and be poor.

'Egeria' was one of the goddesses of prophecy: Pope's Tory friends have
become the mystic descendants of the great Romans by virtue of their
powers of mind and largeness of soul; the floor of the little grotto
becomes 'sacred' because of their presence and that of the ancient goddesses. In fancy the poet occasionally saw himself as a 'Muse-inspired
dreamer beside his trickling spring' (Bracher, *op. cit.*) or even as Apollo,
the Greek god of Poetry. On a visit to the poet at Twickenham, the nine
accomplished and beautiful Misses Lisle of Crux-Easton are reported to
have amused themselves 'by standing on niches in the Grotto as the Nine
Muses; Pope being placed in the midst, as Apollo' (Note, p. 818 in John

his poetry grows richer and even more complex in the new sphere of satire indicates how Pope's relationship with the Muse of Poetry was a developing, many-sided and emotionally satisfying experience. He saw himself as committed to her service, and although he recognised his own passion sometimes as a kind of madness, his conscious dedication to the Muse works simultaneously to ennoble his verse. Describing poets in his *Epistle to Augustus* (1737) as

> (upon a Poet's word)   358
> Of all mankind, the creatures most absurd

Pope presents himself as continually 'renouncing' poetry, as an addict will from time to time try to give up drugs or drink: the Muse is equated here with deplorable folly, and the withdrawal symptoms take the form of a 'raging Fit' and a mad desire for the ink and paper by which the sufferer can at once satisfy and prolong it. Yet in the *Epilogue to the Satires* (1738), the beauty and fiery energy of the Muse appearing 'Diadem'd, with Rays divine' seem to burn in the poem, lifting Pope's claims for his own poetry from rhetorical gesture to recognisable truth:

> Ye tinsel Insects! whom a Court maintains,   220
> That counts your Beauties only by your Stains,
> Spin all your Cobwebs o'er the Eye of Day!
> The Muse's wing shall brush you all away . . .
>
> Truth guards the Poet, sanctifies the line,   246
> And makes Immortal, Verse as mean as mine.

Poetry has become more than a source of personal pleasure, or mental and physical relief: it has provided Pope with a responsible public role. In the *Epilogue to the Satires*, Pope's friend declares him to be 'strangely' proud in his professed sympathy 'for all mankind': there is implied a suggestion that the poet's attitude is odd, fanatic, even paranoiac. Pope's answer is that he believes himself to be divinely directed in writing satire (lines 203–15 of Dialogue II). We might trace his dedicated, almost obsessive desire to see order reign in English public and cultural life to the fact of his own misshapenness: his art had given him the

---

Butt (ed.), *Poems of Pope* (1963, 1965)). A short poem in which Pope celebrated this episode was published after his death, in 1750. It was perhaps an example of the kind of flight of fancy a stern moralist must deny himself in his public life and published poetry.

means to express the first, and relieve and compensate for the second.

Pope's standards certainly take in more than a merely personal code, they derive from ideas generally held in his time about the universe and man's place in it, and they are applied by him to all kinds of experience and situation. His feeling for 'correctness', for shapeliness and proper perspectives in literature extended as he matured, to penetrate every aspect of his experience. It influenced his view of the arts of architecture, painting and landscape gardening as much as his opinion of the moral responsibility of each individual to use his inherited or acquired wealth in a reasonable manner, and to order his personal and religious life according to a generally accepted code of sense and decorum. As a result, his poetry (developing over a period of forty years during which he never ceased to write or revise his writing) continually takes in new ground.

The Muse of Poetry makes her final appearance in Pope's unfinished epic poem, *Brutus*. Here he attempts the high rhetoric of the epic mode, the only one appropriate to the writing of 'spotless' poetry. He adopts a form he has not used before, the blank verse line of Milton's *Paradise Lost*:

> The Patient Chief, who lab'ring long, arriv'd
> On Britain's Shore and brought with fav'ring Gods
> Arts Arms and Honour to her Ancient Sons:
> Daughter of Memory! from elder Time
> Recall: and me, with Britain's Glory fir'd,
> Snatch to thy Holy Hill of spotless Bay,
> My Country's Poet, to record her Fame.

Pope had proved himself to possess the intellectual, moral and technical equipment for epic poetry: breadth of vision, firmly-held religious values, a lively patriotism, the ability to deal concisely with massive materials, the mastery of descriptive skills, of tone, of rhetoric, the perfect control of a chosen verse-form – all that must be possessed by a poet who hoped to follow Milton and rival 'the Bards whom none e'er match'd before'. The writing of a great English epic poem was to be the culmination of Pope's poetic career, prepared for through a lifetime of mental and technical exercise. And yet the project of writing an epic to England's glory was abandoned. This must interest anyone who looks attentively at the fragment quoted above, and notices how elements of

Pope's greatest and most characteristic work – the complex ambiguities, the caustic humour, the ironies – have been jettisoned in order to sustain the high grandeur Pope admired in *Paradise Lost* and had himself perfected in translating *The Iliad* into couplet verse, believing that tone appropriate to the epic mode.

In this fragment the Muse is given her formal ancestry: she is addressed as the 'Daughter of Memory' and begged to recall Brutus's exploits in establishing the Roman arts of civilisation in Britain, sanctifying at the same time Pope's efforts to become England's national poet. All this is appropriate to the solemn tone Pope adopts in these opening lines. In the eighteenth century the highest acclaim was reserved for the kind of distinction, the 'sublimity', Milton had achieved in *Paradise Lost*: evidently Pope wished to be seen as soaring at last above the 'meaner Care' and 'meaner Song' that had preoccupied him too long. It is interesting and surely significant that this poem, which would necessarily have devalued all that he had previously written (and knew to be great poetry) was abandoned and left unfinished. This is evidence of Pope's integrity: when his wish

> to pour out all myself, as plain
> As downright *Shippen*, or as old *Montagne*

came into conflict with his ambition for permanent glory of the Miltonic kind, it was the epic that was abandoned. Today, we are more prepared than were Pope's contemporaries to acknowledge the epic quality in the poems he did write, notably *The Dunciad*.

'I was never so concerned about my works as to vindicate them in print', wrote the poet in the Preface to his published *Works* in 1717,

believing, if any thing was good, it would defend itself, and what was bad could never be defended . . . If this volume perish, let it serve as a warning to the Critics, not to take too much pains for the future to destroy such things as will die of themselves; and a *Memento mori* to some of my vain contemporaries the Poets, to teach them that, when real merit is wanting, it avails nothing to have been encouraged by the great, commended by the eminent, and favoured by the public in general.

In the chapters that follow this Introductory, it is intended to let Pope's poetry 'defend' itself, freed of the handicaps and hindrances that generally discourage or irk new readers of eigh-teenth-century poetry. It is a very special pleasure to acknowledge with gratitude in this connection the contributions made to my own understanding of Pope by the late Upali Amarasinghe, by Robin Mayhead, H. W. Piper, Ruth Waterhouse, and by my students at Peradeniya and at Macquarie whose several responses to my views of particular poems have helped to shape this book.

'The liberty of Borrowing'

'I wou'd beg your opinion too', wrote Pope to his friend Walsh on 2 July 1706, inviting comment on the Pastorals he had sent him, 'as to another point: It is how far the liberty of *Borrowing* may extend? ... A mutual commerce makes Poetry flourish; but then Poets like Merchants, shou'd repay with something of their own what they take from others, not like Pyrates, make prize of all they meet.'

The poet who deliberately inaugurated his career by 'trying the sylvan strains' of pastoral poetry necessarily found himself indebted to predecessors whose success in the form had made it a genre or established 'kind' of verse, and whose practice had set a pattern. 'Among the moderns, their success has been greatest who have most endeavoured to make [Theocritus and Virgil] their pattern', wrote Pope in his *Discourse on Pastoral Poetry* (1709). 'The most considerable Genius appears in the famous Tasso, and our Spenser.' Written at the age of sixteen, these words indicate the poet's early application to the demanding art of composing within a form, just as his anxious inquiry of Walsh reveals the care with which he strove to integrate his own gifts with the requirements of an established tradition.

Any reader familiar with the classical poetry of his own culture, who has examined the relation of a classical tradition to modern developments from it, will be able to place beside Pope's work examples of poets writing to prescribed patterns. Aware how rarely appears the great talent that can 'snatch a Grace beyond the reach of Art', he is thankful for settled literary traditions that ensure a consistent inheritance of good (if not always great) art. But he can also recall examples of the danger to art of a tradition that has become rigid, unrefreshed by contributions from vigorous and original minds; he will be aware of the deadness and sterility, the temptation to mere imitativeness that conformity breeds. It was part of Pope's luck as a poet that the times suited his temperament; he desired perfection in literature, and reform in political and social life, but revolution in neither. Convinced of the permanent value of the standards that supported the framework of his experience, he set himself to mend and strengthen them by his poetic practice.

In *An Essay on Criticism* (1711) Pope sets out his standards, both of literary creation and of critical practice. The poem summarises the literary doctrines accepted by the best, most cultivated minds of the age, and in doing so provides us with another example of Pope's ability to speak for a literary milieu despite his own combativeness, and the individualism that brought him into bitter opposition with many of its members. The poem illuminates Pope's practice in taking 'the liberty of Borrowing'. Its doctrines are largely derived from established, accepted sources. Nature is presented by Pope as the best guide of the judgment:

> First follow NATURE, and your Judgment frame　　68
> By her just Standard, which is still the same:
> *Unerring* Nature, still divinely bright,
> One *clear, unchang'd*, and *Universal* Light,
> Life, Force, and Beauty, must to all impart,
> At once the *Source*, and *End*, and *Test* of *Art*.
> *Art* from that Fund each *just Supply* provides,
> Works *without Show*, and *without Pomp* presides:
> In some fair Body thus th'informing Soul
> With Spirits feeds, with Vigour fills the whole,
> Each Motion guides, and ev'ry Nerve sustains;
> *It self unseen*, but in th'*Effects* remains.

This, together with the view that the rules derived from the practice of the greatest classical poets have a universal application and need to be constantly studied by the critic –

> Those RULES of old *discover'd*, not *devis'd*,　　88
> Are *Nature* still, but *Nature Methodiz'd*;
> *Nature*, like *Liberty*, is but restrain'd
> By the same Laws which first *herself* ordain'd.
> 　Hear how learn'd *Greece* her useful Rules indites,
> When to repress, and when indulge our Flights:
> High on *Parnassus'* Top her Sons she show'd
> And pointed out those arduous Paths they trod,
> Held from afar, aloft, th'Immortal Prize,
> And urg'd the rest by equal Steps to rise;
> Just *Precepts* thus from great *Examples* giv'n,
> She drew from *them* what they deriv'd from *Heav'n* . . .

> *You* then whose Judgment the right Course wou'd
>   steer,   118
> Know well each ANCIENT's proper *Character*,
> His *Fable, Subject, Scope* in ev'ry Page,
> *Religion, Country, Genius* of his *Age*:
> Without all these at once before your Eyes,
> *Cavil* you may, but never *Criticize* . . .

are opinions Pope had inherited through his traditional literary education. His view that the ideal critic strikes a happy medium between frankness and generosity of spirit –

> Who to a *Friend* his Faults can freely show,   637
> And gladly praise the Merit of a *Foe* . . .

between a care for technical accuracy and the appreciation of an almost unlimited range of excellence –

> Blest with a *Taste* exact, yet unconfin'd;   639
> A *Knowledge* both *of Books* and *Humankind* . . .

that contemporary critical practice at its best recalls and reinstates the high standards of Greece and Augustan Rome –

> . . . *some* there were, among the *sounder Few*   719
> Of those who *less presum'd*, and *better knew*,
> Who durst assert the *juster Ancient Cause*,
> And here *restor'd* Wit's *Fundamental Laws*.
> Such was the Muse, whose Rules and Practice tell,
> *Nature's chief Master-piece is writing well* . . .

all this indicates how faithfully Pope mirrors the belief of his times in the beneficial effects of Reason, Sense, and a Decorum that swerves neither to one extreme nor to another. In small matters as well as in great, Pope submits to tradition: having begun the poem with due reverence to the ancients –

> Still green with Bays each *ancient* Altar stands,   181
> Above the reach of *Sacrilegious* Hands,
> Secure from *Flames*, from *Envy's* fiercer Rage,
> Destructive *War*, and all-involving *Age*.
> See, from *each Clime* the Learn'd their Incense bring;
> Hear, in *all Tongues* consenting *Paeans* ring!
> In Praise so just, let ev'ry Voice be join'd,
> And fill the *Gen'ral Chorus* of *Mankind*!
> Hail *Bards Triumphant*! born in *happier Days*;
> *Immortal* Heirs of *Universal* Praise!
> Whose Honours with Increase of Ages *grow*,
> As Streams roll down, *enlarging* as they flow!

he ends it with a disciple's graceful praise of a friend and contemporary –

> *Walsh*, – the Muse's Judge and Friend,   729
> Who justly knew to blame or to commend;
> To Failings *mild*, but *zealous* for Desert;
> The *clearest Head*, and the *sincerest Heart*.

But with all this, there is a great deal in the *Essay* that is unmistakably Pope's own, and it is glimpsed chiefly in the imaginative
range of metaphor used in the presentation of argument and ideas.

The style Pope adopts in the *Essay* was to become characteristic
of him – smooth, ratiocinative, conversational, the critical maxims
dressed appropriately in contemporary metaphor and idiom:

> But most by *Numbers* judge a Poet's Song,   337
> And *smooth* or *rough*, with them, is *right* or *wrong*;
> In the bright *Muse* tho' thousand *Charms* conspire,
> Her *Voice* is all these tuneful Fools admire,
> Who *haunt Parnassus* but to please their Ear,
> Not mend their Minds; as some to *Church* repair,
> Not for the *Doctrine*, but the *Musick* there.

The word 'numbers' for Pope and his contemporaries meant
something very close to what we mean by 'rhythm' – conformity
in verse or music, to a certain regular beat or measure. The comparison of 'critics' who judge verse by the regularity of its rhythm
to churchgoers who rate an accomplished choir higher than a
serious preacher, is both apt and witty, reminding the reader that
good literature must instruct as it delights, combining moral and
aesthetic satisfaction in due proportion. At times, however, Pope's
metaphors are not merely comfortably appropriate, but startle us
in a way that recalls his inheritance of the Metaphysicals' conception of 'wit':

> Some praise at Morning what they blame at Night;   430
> But always think the *last* Opinion *right*.
> A Muse by these is like a Mistress us'd,
> This hour she's *idoliz'd*, the next *abus'd* . . .

The laxities of the Restoration (and the example of King Charles
II) had done much to remove from the word 'Mistress' both its
original solid respectability (e.g. the 'Mistress' of the manor) and
the romantic idealism with which it had been imbued by Eliza-
bethan poets writing despairing Petrarchan sonnets to an un-

attainable 'Mistress'. These meanings linger on in the eighteenth and nineteenth centuries, but the situation projected in Pope's lines is implicitly a sexual one and of an irregular kind. Supported by the easy familiarity that must exist between lovers who see one another 'Night' and 'Morning', and by the sexual meanings latent in the words 'used' and 'abused', the surprising metaphor links in the reader's mind certain critical pronouncements on literature with the casual insensitivity a man might display to a woman who illicitly occupies the place of a wife. It does what the true Metaphysical metaphor should do: it sharpens our understanding of the subject under discussion, and alerts us to its several significances. To Pope, who had experienced the mysterious joy of poetic creation in communion with his Muse (see pp. 13–19, critical inconsistency appears to cheapen and brutalise the constant, honourable relationship that should bind a writer to the divine spirit of Poetry.

At times Pope's imagination fires, and throws out an image that flashes a signal of what is to come: as when he alludes to writers who, having figured as wits, poets, and critics, must be content at last to prove themselves mere fools, as

> half-learn'd Witlings, num'rous in our Isle,   40
> As half-form'd Insects on the Banks of *Nile*:
> Unfinish'd Things, one knows not what to call,
> Their Generation's so *equivocal* . . .

When Pope, after a lifetime of warfare with such buzzing 'Insects' as these came to write the fourth Book of *The Dunciad*, he knew what to call them. The ignorant hack, the incompetent critic, the poetaster, the plagiarist figure unforgettably in the undignified forms of a horde of insects and parasites clustering about their Goddess, Dulness, as bees swarm around their queen, their clamour filling the reader's mind as he goes through the poem.

Pope does not hesitate to use homely, everyday similes and metaphors to illustrate critical abstractions: thus,

> For *Wit* and *Judgment* often are at strife,   82
> Tho' meant each other's Aid, like *Man* and *Wife*.

Elsewhere, inferior critics are likened to chemists, who get on at first by imitating the methods of their masters the physicians, and end by bringing the art of medicine into disrepute (lines 108–11). Inferior poets are compared to unskilled painters who hope to

conceal the absence in their work of a central well-defined theme,
with an abundance of decoration and glitter:

> Some to *Conceit* alone their Taste confine,　　　　289
> And glitt'ring Thoughts struck out at ev'ry Line;
> Pleas'd with a Work where nothing's just or fit;
> One *glaring Chaos* and *wild Heap* of *Wit*:
> Poets like Painters, thus, unskill'd to trace
> The *naked Nature* and the *living Grace*,
> With *Gold* and *Jewels* cover ev'ry Part,
> And hide with *Ornaments* their *Want of Art*.

Critics who value style more than sense are pictured as praising

> *Books*, as Women *Men*, for *Dress*.　　　　306

The literary enthusiast is compared to a traveller lost in a decep-
tive mist (line 392), the too-severe critic accused of possessing a
queasy stomach for literature:

> Those *Heads* as *Stomachs* are not sure the best　　　　388
> Which nauseate all, and nothing can digest.

The futile efforts at imaginative creation of certain incorrigible
versifiers are pilloried in four lines:

> Still *run on* Poets in a raging Vein,　　　　606
> Ev'n to the Dregs and *Squeezings* of the *Brain*;
> Strain out the last, dull droppings of their Sense,
> And Rhyme with all the *Rage* of *Impotence*!

Presenting this inferior verse as indistinguishable from the (unsuc-
cessful) processes of winepress or kitchen, bedroom and lavatory,
it is obvious that the poet has enjoyed his search for the exact
word that will suit his purposes – we note the wicked accuracy of
the alliterative, onomatopoeic 'last / dull / droppings', and the
delight in his own superior powers reflected in the easy linking of
'Rhyme' with '*Rage*'. Passages such as these look forward to the
richness and energy of the sewer-games in Book II of *The Dunciad*,
and exemplify the truth that for a great poet all aspects of life
provide raw material for art, nothing need be left out that illuminates a theme or an experience.

　　Another aspect of the *Essay on Criticism* that bears the stamp
of Pope's individual interests is that of versification, or 'numbers'.
We can see the fledgling poet demonstrating his skill in the choice
of words, in a passage that makes the movement of the verse
hasten, pant, labour or take wing:

'Tis not enough no Harshness gives Offence,   364
The *Sound* must seem an *Eccho* to the *Sense*.
Soft is the Strain when *Zephyr* gently blows,
And the *smooth Stream* in *smoother Numbers* flows;
But when loud Surges lash the sounding Shore,
The *hoarse, rough Verse* shou'd like the *Torrent* roar.
When *Ajax* strives, some Rock's vast Weight to throw,
The Line too *labours*, and the Words move *slow*;
Not so, when swift *Camilla* scours the Plain,
Flies o'er th'unbending Corn, and skims along the Main.

These lines deserve the closest attention from every hopeful or practising poet who uses the medium of the English language. Pope's virtuosity in skilfully varying the basic rhythm of iambic pentameter to suit his immediate aims does not depend exclusively on the exploitation of sounds, e.g. the use of muted 's' sounds in lines 366–7, or the lengthening of vowel sounds in lines 370–1. The sense of what is being said produces variations within variations, as when our visualisation of the upstanding corn reinforces the resistance offered by the words themselves to the rapid movements of the flying nymph in line 373, seeming thereby to accelerate the speed she achieves after she has passed over it. In another passage we find Pope expressing his amusement at the clumsiness and tediousness of contemporary poets, who

ring round the same *unvary'd Chimes*,   348
With sure *Returns* of still *expected Rhymes*.
Where-e'er you find *the cooling Western Breeze*,
In the next Line, it *whispers thro' the Trees*;
In *Chrystal Streams* with *pleasing Murmurs creep*,
The Reader's threaten'd (not in vain) with *Sleep*.
Then, at the *last*, and *only* Couplet fraught
With some *unmeaning* Thing they call a *Thought*,
A *needless Alexandrine* ends the Song,
That like a wounded Snake, drags its slow length along.

All this is exhilarating to read, evidence of a vigorous, growing talent and a mind that delights in intelligent mockery. Pope's raillery in the second passage is just criticism expressed with poise and wit, and includes (in the last couplet) a demonstration of the deadening effect of an unnecessary poetic device: fair warning that this critic knows what he is talking about.

Another feature of *An Essay on Criticism* that points forward to later, greater successes, is Pope's skill at portraiture. An

amusing portrait of his testy contemporary, the critic and playwright John Dennis, is condensed into three telling lines –

> But *Appius* reddens at each Word you speak,   585
> And *stares, Tremendous!* with a *threatning Eye,*
> Like some *fierce Tyrant* in *Old Tapestry!*

Another six give us a view of

> the Bookful Blockhead, ignorantly read   612
> With *Loads* of *Learned Lumber* in his Head,
> With his own Tongue still edifies his Ears,
> And always *List'ning to Himself* appears.
> All Books he reads, and all he reads assails,
> From *Dryden's Fables* down to *Durfey's Tales.*

Like the portrait of 'the Man of Ross' in one of Pope's later
Satires, we have in contrast to these his pictures of the ideal
critic in the lines quoted as passage A in Chapter 1, and in lines
631–42:

> But where's the Man, who Counsel *can* bestow,
> Still *pleas'd* to *teach*, and yet not *proud* to *know?*
> Unbiass'd, or by *Favour* or by *Spite*;
> Not *dully prepossest*, nor *blindly right*;
> Tho' Learn'd, well-bred; and tho' well-bred, sincere;
> Modestly bold, and Humanly severe?
> Who to a *Friend* his Faults can freely show,
> And gladly praise the merit of a *Foe?*
> Blest with a *Taste* exact, yet unconfin'd;
> A *Knowledge* both of *Books* and *Humankind*;
> *Gen'rous Converse*; a *Soul* exempt from *Pride*;
> And *Love to Praise*, with *Reason* on his Side?

To Pope the good critic was a good judge, a view that places a
high value on the careful process by which virtues are weighed
against faults before a verdict is delivered. Such a critic alone
could experience the *generous pleasure* yielded by good literature,
for such a critic alone would view a work with the trained and
sympathetic eye a serious writer hopes for in his reader. These are
terms that lead us back consistently and continually to Pope's own
poetic practice. Tirelessly attentive to rhythmic effects and visual
detail, endlessly fastidious in his choice of word and phrase,
Pope's poetry yet seeks the perfection of harmony and wholeness
rather than of striking particularity. At its best it attains the ideal
of true 'Wit' as expressed in an *Essay on Criticism* –

> *True Wit* is *Nature* to Advantage drest,   297
> What oft was *Thought*, but ne'er so well *Exprest*,

where

> . . . *Nature moves,* and *Rapture warms* the Mind,   236

combining graceful and correct expression with sense and deep feeling, blending traditional, contemporary and individual elements to form a pleasing and harmonious whole.

3

'Common Town-Wits and downright Country Fools'

'I have now chang'd the scene from the Town to the Country; from *Will's* Coffee-House to *Windsor* Forest', wrote Pope to Wycherley on 26 October 1705:

I find no other difference than this, betwixt the common Town-Wits, and the downright Country Fools; that the first are pertly in the Wrong, with a little more Flourish and Gaiety, and the last neither in the Right nor the Wrong, but confirmed in a stupid, settled Medium betwixt both . . . Ours are a sort of modest, inoffensive People, who neither have Sense, nor pretend to any, but enjoy a jovial sort of Dulness. They are commonly known in the World by the Name of honest, civil Gentlemen. They live much as they ride, at random; a kind of hunting Life, pursuing with earnestness and hazard, something not worth the catching; never in the way, nor out of it. I can't but prefer Solitude to the Company of all these . . .

The gap between a cultivated Augustan and a mere 'honest, civil Gentleman' of town or country could be wide. Pope's comic exaggerations were intended to amuse his friend, but his letter projects two life-styles distinct from one another and completely different from his own, which was that of a cultured urbanite. In a poem written ten years afterwards to amuse another friend, Miss Theresa Blount, Pope caricatured rural life once more, picturing the boredom suffered by a lovely 'nymph' who leaves the gaieties of a Coronation in London to bury herself and her charms in the country:

> She went, to plain-work, and to purling brooks,   11
> Old-fashion'd halls, dull aunts, and croaking rooks,
> She went from Op'ra, park, assembly, play,
> To morning walks, and pray'rs three hours a day;
> To pass her time 'twixt reading and Bohea*,
> To muse, and spill her solitary Tea,
> Or o'er cold coffee trifle with the spoon,
> Count the slow clock, and dine exact at noon;
> Divert her eyes with pictures in the fire,

* Chinese black tea.

Hum half a tune, tell stories to the squire;
Up to her godly garret after sev'n,
There starve and pray, for that's the way to heav'n.
　　　　　From *An Epistle to a Young Lady, on
　　　　　her leaving the Town, after the
　　　　　Coronation* (1717)

From the flurry of activity suggested by the crowded line 13, the verse settles down to an untroubled rhythm that regularly alternates an unbroken line with another as regularly divided in the middle, illustrating Pope's own maxim that the sound must seem 'an *Eccho* to the *Sense*' by permitting us to 'hear' the lively irregularities of a London season give way to a monotonous country routine. Since such agonies of boredom must have some relief, Pope pictures his pretty friend amusing herself by flirting with a local swain:

　　Some Squire, perhaps, you take delight to rack;　　　23
　　Whose game is Whisk*, whose treat a toast in sack†,
　　Who visits with a gun, presents you birds,
　　Then gives a smacking buss‡, and cries – No words!
　　Or with his hound comes hollowing from the stable,
　　Makes love with nods, and knees beneath a table;
　　Whose laughs are hearty, tho' his jests are coarse,
　　And loves you best of all things – but his horse.

　* Whist, the card-game.　　　† White wine.　　　‡ Kiss.

We recognise the 'honest' sportsman of Pope's letter to Wycherley, to whose jovial stupidity the poet had preferred solitude. The slight change in the verse-movement from one kind of regularity to another as the Squire enters the poem is appropriate to the sense of what is being said: his courtship of the young woman introduces some small variation into her tiresomely regulated life. But the change is one that opens the way to satire as the poet examines the Squire's mode of courtship – 'Whose game is . . . *Whisk*! / whose treat . . . a toast *in sack*! / Who visits . . . with a *gun*! / presents you . . . *birds*!' Every delicate attention that forms a traditional part of sophisticated lovemaking, for which the cultivated wit (Pope) would have drawn on a personal repertoire of refinements, is grasped eagerly by this yokel and damaged as surely as if he had stamped upon it with his clumsy boots. Pope's picture of the hunting squire noisily approaching the boudoir direct from the stable, his hound scrambling at his heels, is exact and pleasant comedy, but the next line is something more: innocent of the subtleties possible between those who understand the arts of writing and conversation, compliment and courtesy, the Squire's love-making places him among the animals, his natural sphere the stable and not the salon.

The Rape of the Lock (1712, 1714), a poem that takes as its theme the confused values of a brilliant and fashionable social world, gives us (besides much else) a portrait of a 'common Town-Wit' that may be placed beside the 'downright Country Fool' we have just been examining. Sir Plume is a fop (his name betrays his love of fine feathers). Chosen to present Belinda's 'case' to the Baron, and to demand the return of her stolen lock of hair,

> (*Sir Plume*, of *Amber Snuff-box* justly vain,   123
> And the nice* Conduct of a *clouded Cane*)
> With earnest Eyes, and round unthinking Face,
> He first the Snuff-box open'd, then the Case,
> And thus broke out – 'My Lord, why, what the Devil?
> Z – ds! damn the Lock! fore Gad, you must be civil!
> Plague on't! 'tis past a Jest – nay prithee, Pox!
> Give her the Hair' – he spoke, and rapp'd his Box.
>
> * Fastidious.

Despite the discouraging signs of vanity and foppery presented in Sir Plume's expensive cane and snuff-box, and the teasing reminder that he opened the snuff-box first and '*then* the Case', the reader might be led to take hope in the forthright sound of 'And thus broke out'; Sir Plume might still, in spite of indications to the contrary, prove a competent advocate. But as soon as he opens his mouth, the 'case' is as good as lost. Where the country squire cried hastily, 'No words!' and relied on nods and nudges to convey his feelings, the town 'wit' can only expostulate. As one oath succeeds another our amusement at the poverty of the knight's vocabulary turns into amazement at the variety of Pope's, and there is elegant sarcasm in the Baron's reply:

> It grieves me much (reply'd the Peer again)   131
> Who speaks so well shou'd ever speak in vain.

Sir Plume deserves the rebuke: his diction is the common inarticulacy of the upper-class fool, mixed with equally common and quite unjustified self-assurance. Pope's scorn for him is blended with an odd admiration, a kind of wonder that his species exists. This fusion of scorn and wonder pervades the whole of *The Rape of the Lock*, as Belinda floats sun-like over clouds of envy and worship to the poem's appointed end.

The poem's title, with its built-in reminiscences of heroic events like the rape of Lucrece by Tarquin and the abduction of Helen of Sparta by the Trojan prince Paris, conveys to us immediately that Pope is writing in the mock-heroic mode. Dedicated to Miss Arabella Fermor, victim of the original insult from Lord Petre, the poem politely assures her that its coquettish heroine resembles her in nothing but beauty and the experience of a similar loss of a lock of hair. However, the poem's whole purpose is to say something subtle and serious – yet not too direct – to such as Miss Fermor, about the social values that control the life of the society beauty. *The Rape of the Lock* focuses in this way upon society itself; wittily treating a trivial social quarrel as if it had been a second Trojan War, Pope hints at the need for better order and proportion in social attitudes and social behaviour.

The poem's structure reminds us that at the time of its composition Pope was working on his translation of Homer: it takes the form of a point-by-point miniature version of *The Iliad*, perfect in every detail. The greater poem's reflection is seen in such formal matters as the preparations made for battle by the heroes of the opposing factions. Belinda pays ritual devotions to the '*Cosmetic* Pow'rs', and with their aid we see how

> awful Beauty puts on all its Arms;   I, 139
> The Fair each moment rises in her Charms,
> Repairs her Smiles, awakens ev'ry Grace,
> And calls forth all the Wonders of her Face;
> Sees by Degrees a purer Blush arise,
> And keener Lightnings quicken in her Eyes.

As Belinda increases the deadly effect of her beauty with the aid of careful make-up, we remember certain Olympian deities in *The Iliad* who raised the mortal talents of their favourites to superhuman heights on the field of battle. The Baron, for his part, prays to Love, builds an altar of French novels, lights it with torches made of love-letters, sacrifices upon it the souvenirs of previous love-affairs, and raises the flames with passionate sighs. The athletic Games that take place on either side before and during various stages of the classic war are echoed, suitably diminished, in the game of cards that Belinda plays with the Baron and another love-sick admirer. The feasting and ritual libations made to the gods in Homer reappear in *The Rape of the Lock* as ritual chocolate- and coffee-drinking. The act of treachery, the vow of revenge, the speeches of heroes, the intervention of supernatural forces in human affairs, the descent into a gloomy underworld, the sanctification of some precious object or person as a starry constellation – all the familiar classical machinery reappears in Pope's poem, appropriately altered or trimmed to fit the manners and customs of Belinda's social circle.

The language of the poem recalls the epic model continuously, achieving different effects in different contexts. When 'grave Clarissa' points out the value of good humour and good sense in Canto v, we are informed –

> So spoke the Dame, but no Applause ensu'd 35

a line that looks back to Homer's 'So spoke Ulysses, and all the heroes applauded'. The pair of scissors with which the Baron performs his act of treachery is glorified in heroic terms as 'the glitt'ring *Forfex*', 'a two-edg'd Weapon', 'the little Engine' – this is technically known as periphrasis, the device of expressing some idea in a circuitous (and consequently often pompous) manner. By his use of it here Pope is reinforcing his satiric purpose, emphasising the insignificance of the object referred to. But especially interesting and a continuous source of enrichment to the poem are the metaphors that Pope draws for his own use from the epic original, heightening their effect from time to time by means of scriptural allusions.

First, and most striking, of these is the metaphor by which Belinda is seen as a Sun. The allusion is obviously complimentary, for example in Canto i she opens 'Eyes that must eclipse the Day' (14), and in Canto ii she is 'the Rival' of the Sun himself (3). But other meanings soon begin to accumulate around the central complimentary metaphor: as she is as bright and impartial as sunshine, Belinda's gaze indiscriminately shines 'on all alike' (ii, 14). She is the centre of a brilliant solar system of 'wits' and 'belles', – but we cannot have much respect for a social circle in which

> *Snuff*, or the *Fan*, supply each Pause of Chat, iii, 17
> With singing, laughing, ogling, and all that.

Belinda's period of brilliance, like the Sun's, is a strictly limited one, and doomed to end in twilight and darkness. The poem supports this idea by allowing its action to fill the space of a single day, the progress of that day being marked by frequent references to the Sun's position in the sky. The Sun-metaphor has the effect, in this way, of reminding us of Belinda's humanity and mortality, even as it expands our impression of her beauty and personal magnetism.

Secondly, Belinda is compared to creative divinity. When she takes up her cards and begins the game of Ombre, she becomes for a moment God creating the Universe: the lines

> The skilful Nymph reviews her Force with Care;   III, 45
> *Let Spades be Trumps!* she said, and Trumps they were

parody the verses in the Book of Genesis that describe the Creation – 'And God said, *Let there be light*; and there was Light.' In any case, from the poem's very start Belinda has been presented as a goddess to whose greater glory all nations on earth render 'cosmetic' tributes, to deck whom the elephant and the tortoise are sacrificed and

> Transform'd to *Combs*, the speckled and the white.   I, 136

Belinda's nightly ritual of curling her hair has been nothing less than a voluntary submission to pain and discomfort for the benefit of mankind:

> Was it for this you took such constant Care   IV, 97
> The *Bodkin*, *Comb*, and *Essence* to prepare;
> For this your Locks in Paper-Durance bound,
> For this with tort'ring Irons wreath'd around?
> For this with Fillets strain'd your tender Head,
> And bravely bore the double Loads of Lead?

and the theft of her hair is treated as an act of sacrilege, its final elevation to the skies making her a permanent symbol (like the planet Venus) of Love.

Thirdly, Belinda is presented as a hero preparing for an epic battle, the war between the sexes for ultimate mastery. She has nurtured the disputed lock of hair, intending it as a manoeuvre of deliberate provocation 'to the Destruction of Mankind' (II, 19). 'Lucid Squadrons' of sylphs help her in her campaign (II, 56), their special duties including the defence of her attractive person

and its 'sev'nfold Fence', her petticoat (II, 117–22). Her bodkin
has a pedigree similar to that given by Homer to Agamemnon's
sceptre. Her victory in the card-game is a military triumph, and
in the larger battle for sexual mastery that develops from and
finally envelops it, Pope's witty contemporary play upon the
sexual meaning of the word 'death' equates heroic valour with
sexual consummation –

> See fierce *Belinda* on the *Baron* flies,   v, 75
> With more than usual Lightning in her Eyes;
> Nor fear'd the Chief th'unequal Fight to try,
> Who sought no more than on his Foe to die.

Their battle is 'unequal' because of her divine nature, as evi-
denced by the 'Lightning' in her eyes; the Baron is a mere mortal. But it is 'unequal' too because Belinda is a woman, and
physically weaker than her aggressor: there is a suggestion here
that the Baron's act has been cowardly and un'heroic'. And yet
he is in his own way a hero, asking no more than the fate Spar-
tan mothers demanded for their gallant sons, death in battle.
Since his 'Foe' is a woman, however, a battle with her can only
be a sexual one: the Baron is seeking the pleasurable 'death' that
comes to every happy and successful lover. In this way the metaphors reinforce and contradict one another, building in concert a
powerful impression of secret, unacknowledged passion of a sexual
nature underlying the ritual formalities of social etiquette. The
Baron's action has brought these feelings out into the open;
Belinda may call him a 'rapacious' monster, but he is more
natural, less artificial than she is. In their battle, as Clarissa
rightly points out, 'victory' can only lie in the development of
sensible adult attitudes to one another,

> since, alas! frail Beauty must decay,   v, 25
> Curl'd or uncurl'd, since Locks will turn to grey,
> Since painted, or not painted, all shall fade,
> And she who scorns a Man, must die a Maid;
> What then remains, but well our Pow'r to use,
> And keep good Humour still whate'er we lose?

not in childish tantrums, or coquettish dreams of 'Conquests' yet
to come.

Fourth, Pope uses the metaphor of religious ritual to surround
Belinda and all she does with an aura of light and power. Her

life is dedicated to the decoration and worship of her own 'divine' beauty:

> And now, unveiled, the *Toilet* stands display'd,   I, 121
> Each Silver Vase in mystic Order laid.
> First, rob'd in White, the Nymph intent adores
> With Head uncover'd, the *Cosmetic* Pow'rs.
> A heav'nly Image in the Glass appears,
> To that she bends, to that her Eyes she rears.

The details regarding the 'unveiling' of the dressing table, the 'mystic' nature of the arrangements upon it, the white garment worn by the priestess, the baring of her head, the use of the word 'adoration', create the atmosphere of a religious ceremony, subtly reinforced by an incantatory rhythm – 'To *that* she bends, to *that* her Eyes she rears . . .' The reader might be amused by the distortion of Belinda's values, but he cannot avoid being impressed by the solemnity of the processes described, and surprised by their splendour into entering at least a little sympathetically into her feelings about herself and her world.

And while these metaphors work, singly and in subtle combinations, to elevate Belinda's status and surround her with 'divine' glory, Pope reminds us that she is always and at all times merely human. When her eyes flash Jove-like 'living Lightnings', it is because she is behaving like a spoilt child in a tantrum, or perhaps she has been using cosmetics to brighten her eyes. Her frailties are those of her sex, her soul is 'taintable', her chastity is preserved by her own vanity and fickleness, her emotions are plainly obvious to all: for when she is about to lose a trivial game of cards, we are told that

> the Blood the Virgin's Cheek forsook,   III, 89
> A livid Paleness spreads o'er all her Look;

and when she wins, she 'exults' (III, 99). Her lament for her stolen lock of hair is characteristically exaggerated –

> Oh had I rather unadmir'd remain'd   IV, 153
> In some lone Isle, or distant *Northern* Land;
> Where the gilt *Chariot* never marks the Way,
> Where none learn *Ombre**, none e'er taste *Bohea*!
> There kept my Charms conceal'd from mortal Eye,
> Like Roses that in Desarts bloom and die . . .

> * A card game played by three persons, with
> forty cards.

She resents Clarissa's lecture on the value of good sense, since it implies criticism of her own behaviour (v, 36). Admired by all, Belinda is a permanent potential victim, one false step taken socially and her 'fall' will be as final as that of the society beauties whose reputations supply each 'Pause of Chat' at Hampton Court, where

> *Britain*'s Statesmen oft the Fall foredoom III, 5
> Of Foreign Tyrants, and of Nymphs at home.

The social pressure upon Belinda to maintain her stance of innocent, 'unspoiled' coquettishness is very great; she must never yield to natural feeling, never give her heart. Hence the extraordinary uproar she creates over the loss of a lock of hair. She knows, and her friend Thaletris unctuously reminds her, that her reputation will never be the same again (because it will be assumed that she gave the lock willingly as a love-token):

> Methinks already I your Tears survey, IV, 107
> Already hear the horrid things they say,
> Already see you a degraded Toast,
> And all your Honour in a Whisper lost!
> How shall I, then, your helpless Fame defend?
> 'Twill then be Infamy to seem your Friend!

Belinda's humanity, her childishness, her defencelessness and vulnerability in an amoral society dedicated (under its false, superficial gallantry) to her destruction, give the poem its peculiar tension. Grave issues underlie its brilliant, smooth surface, and the liveliness of Pope's comic wit emphasises their seriousness without weighing the poem down with didactic moralising.

The metaphoric richness of the poem's language is intimately connected with another kind of richness, that of rhythm and verse texture. The precise rhyming of the couplet form and the patterned formalities of Pope's verse paragraphs chime in well with the epic dignity he wants to recreate – even if only in mockery. The suitability of couplet verse to the special needs of argument and ratiocination fits it well to his purpose, that of pointing out and recalling good sense. The pause, or *caesura*, that occurs in or towards the centre of a line is especially effective in satiric passages in which Pope strives after telling antithesis; as in Canto II, when Belinda's guardian sylph meditates on the nature of the unknown danger that threatens her:

This Day, black Omens threat the brightest Fair   II, 100
That e'er deserv'd a watchful Spirit's Care;
Some dire Disaster, or by Force, or Slight,
But what, or where, the Fates have wrapt in Night.
Whether the Nymph shall break *Diana*'s Law,
Or some frail *China* Jar receive a Flaw,
Or stain her Honour, or her new Brocade,
Forget her Pray'rs, or miss a Masquerade,
Or lose her Heart, or Necklace, at a Ball;
Or whether Heav'n has doom'd that *Shock* must fall.

The rhythm implies a series of equations and matched proposi-
tions, yet our good sense insists that the equations are false, their
juxtapositions absurd. The loss of chastity cannot (reason argues)
be placed on the same level as the chipping of a china vase, however precious; yet Pope places them so that the two disparate,
warring ideas share a single couplet, and balance one another.
The satire originates in the way Pope draws on a framework of
traditional, accepted moral values, alluding constantly to them in
a series of ironic contexts, and making skilful use of the antithetical, balancing pattern the couplet affords him. Nor is the
irony of the passage a simple matter of contrasting moral values
with social trivia: the '*China* Jar' is an expensive ornament,
Belinda's 'Brocade' a new and pretty dress, a 'Masquerade' an
event that depends for its success upon clever deception, a 'Necklace' is worn in order to enhance a woman's beauty. The antitheses suggest that Belinda's morality functions on similar levels –
it is merely a decorative, pretty deception, a public advertisement
of its owner's market value, an enhancement of her physical
attractions. This kind of verbal richness is made possible by the
detail Pope packs into the basic antithetical contrasts that the
couplet's structure allows him to make.

Another, related, use of the rhymed couplet is that of rhymed
catalogue:

Not louder Shrieks to pitying Heav'n are cast,   III, 157
When Husbands or when Lap-dogs breathe their last,
Or when rich *China* Vessels, fal'n from high,
In glittring Dust and painted Fragments lie!

A string of trivial incidents are linked together – the death of a
spaniel, the loss of a lock of hair, the shattering of a porcelain
vase. These are contrasted with a real loss, the death of a husband. And the line that links 'Husbands' with 'Lap-dogs' and the

catalogue that joins them all incongruously together indicate briefly that Belinda's circle is not devoid of feeling, but that its emotion is mistakenly and indiscriminately lavished on trivial and important matters alike. And yet, again, the irony here is not as simple as it seems at first glance: a 'China jar' was a contemporary symbol and synonym for female chastity, and little dogs were cherished in innumerable boudoirs as substitutes for the affection of a busy or philandering husband. The observant eye that notes how an admired and expensive piece of porcelain ends in mere 'glittering Dust and painted Fragments' on the floor might be reflecting on the fragility of female chastity – but it might also be remarking on the surprising fact that 'there's nothing much to it, after all'. And although spaniels might seem to figure too importantly in their mistresses' affections, perhaps it is because they have to substitute for their absent masters – or because those masters are, in any case, so spaniel-like that it's hard to tell man and dog apart? Pope presents the reader with a series of enticing possibilities, each one involving him in moral judgments of one kind or another. An interesting catalogue occurs in Canto I, where among the luxurious effects of Belinda's dressing table we come upon one incongruous object –

> This Casket *India*'s glowing Gems unlocks,   133
> And all *Arabia* breathes from yonder Box.
> The Tortoise here and Elephant unite,
> Transform'd to *Combs*, the speckled and the white.
> Here Files of Pins extend their shining Rows,
> Puffs, Powders, Patches, Bibles, Billet-doux.

The word 'Bibles' is linked alliteratively to Belinda's love-letters, and as usually happens with alliteration, the similarity of the linked sounds leads us to associate the objects they name. But the passage is presented from Belinda's point of view, not ours. She is the goddess everyone worships, it is in her confused mind that her Bible and her love-letters share equal importance, and on her dressing table that they are thrown together with other alliteratively linked objects – 'Puffs, Powders, Patches', cosmetics that will form part of her weaponry in the forthcoming battle.

This poem, which is in its way a meditation upon the importance of proper social and human perspectives, gains weight and added metaphorical richness from Pope's habit of allusiveness, the skill and deliberateness with which he takes the 'liberty of *Borrow-*

ing'. The sylphs who surround Belinda and protect her 'honour' are Pope's imaginative invention, but they originate in Rosicrucian philosophy, and if we have recognised their kinship with Homer's Olympians, we must also note their evident descent from the bright spirits of Milton's *Paradise Lost*. The sylphs and their enemies the gnomes were a late addition to the poem, which was first composed and circulated without the benefit of their presence. Their addition in the later version does a great deal to support the 'mock-epic' aspects of the poem, especially our sense of a Heaven which the sylphs inhabit, a Hell that belongs to the gnomes, and an Earth peopled by the *beau monde* of Belinda's circle. The sheer verbal beauty of Pope's evocation of the sylphs sheds a delicacy on the poem as a whole, making it glitter and tremble in the imagination as if it were something fragile and transparent. Actually, the poem and the imagination that created it are tough, and controlled with the utmost care. How tough, how controlled, we can see if we examine in detail the passage in which Ariel (Belinda's guardian sylph) describes the punishments meted out to a sylph who neglects his 'duties'. Ariel's voice becomes in some indefinable way the voice of Milton's archangel Michael, and the tortures he describes are the tortures of the damned:

> Whatever Spirit, careless of his Charge,   II, 123
> His Post neglects, or leaves the Fair at large,
> Shall feel sharp Vengeance soon o'ertake his Sins,
> Be stopt in *Vials*, or transfixt with *Pins*;
> Or plung'd in Lakes of bitter *Washes** lie,
> Or wedg'd whole Ages in a *Bodkin*'s Eye:
> *Gums* and *Pomatums* shall his Flight restrain,
> While clog'd he beats his silken Wings in vain;
> Or Alom-*Stypticks*† with contracting Power
> Shrink his thin Essence like a rivell'd Flower.
> Or as *Ixion* fix'd, the Wretch shall feel
> The giddy Motion of the whirling Mill,
> In Fumes of burning Chocolate shall glow,
> And tremble at the Sea that froaths below!

    * Face-lotions.   † Astringents.

There is here a special kind of tension: between the deliberate cruelty of the punishments described, the acute physical pain they would inflict upon a tiny, delicate creature such as Pope has created in our imagination, and the comic insignificance of those punishments from a human point of view. The tortures of the

Inferno are transformed into miniature versions, imprisonment
in a scent-bottle, drowning in a puddle of spilled face-lotion,
entrapment in an unwashed comb or the eye of a bodkin, impale-
ment on a safety pin, irritation by a drop of astringent liquid, or
the agony of being bound on the whirling wheel of a bean-grinder
and menaced by the prospect of falling at any moment into the
foaming hot chocolate that the ladies sip. The fact that these
instruments of 'torture' are part of everyday feminine existence
makes them precisely appropriate to the punishment of wrong-
doers guilty of neglecting feminine concerns; but they impart, at
the same time, a sinister air to the feminine diversions of sewing,
dressing and chocolate-drinking. As Gulliver found in the Land of
Brobdignag, the most trivial object holds hidden menace; and
even while the poet is obviously delighting in the detail of his
miniature Inferno, putting his talent and imagination to work to
create delicate rather than grand effects, the picture he draws
reinforces his moral intention. It underlines, through its deliberate
play on minimised size and degree, the theme of proper perspective and accurate, reasoned judgment.

The sylphs are themselves extensions of human character,
Belinda's in particular, and of womankind in general. Like the
heroine of the poem, they are decorative, graceful, quick-moving:
Pope suggests that they are also fickle, unstable, superficial and
selfish. Their concerns are identical with hers: concentrating on
outward appearances, they encourage and justify her coquettishness and vanity –

> Our humbler Province is to tend the Fair,   II, 91
> Not a less pleasing, tho' less glorious Care.
> To save the Powder from too rude a Gale,
> Nor let th'imprisoned Essences exhale . . .
> Nay oft, in Dreams, Invention we bestow,
> To change a *Flounce*, or add a *Furbelo*.

They direct their major efforts to the protection of her 'honour',
by which is meant not so much 'modesty', nor even 'virginity',
as 'public reputation'. When Belinda loses control of her emotions,
and gives way to anger and resentment, the sylphs join in the fray,
or perch on bodkins to get a better view (v, 55–6). But when she
actually falls in love and is, presumably, in real need of spiritual
guidance, the sylphs fall silent and retire (III, 139–46). Presented
as miniature versions of Homer's Olympians, the sylphs gain dig-

nity from the comparison, in much the same way that Belinda gains stature from being likened to a goddess. Equipped with the power of flight and of penetration into human hearts and minds, they are assigned various spheres of duty in the universe; Ariel's description of his kind reveals a fascinating picture of another Chain of Being, complete with orders and degrees, on which the sylphs who protect Belinda and *her* kind have a special and distinctive place (II, 75–100). Like Homer's deities, they are fond of interfering in the affairs of mortals, and in the same way that Venus snatched Paris away in a bright cloud just as he was about to be slain by Achilles, and deposited him on a couch in Priam's palace, the sylphs descend and sit in order of their degree on the picture cards in Belinda's hand (III, 31–6). They deploy themselves around the 'sev'nfold Fence' of her hooped petticoat. Their presence and their guardianship of Belinda give the events Pope describes a mock-importance, a patently false grandeur that helps his satiric intention to succeed. (See pp. 105–8.)

The detail in which the sylphs are drawn is intimately connected with the detail Pope lavishes on certain other subjects, notably the toilette sequence in Canto I and the coffee-drinking ritual in Canto III. All three are treated with a solemnity appropriate to sacred subjects. In Canto I the silver vases of cosmetics are laid out in the 'mystic Order' usually reserved for altar vessels; the curtain is drawn to reveal the altar-cum-dressing table at which Belinda simultaneously presides, worships and officiates; and a solemn, impressive rhythm comically underlines the mistaken code of values that makes Belinda prostrate herself before the reflection of her own beauty. In Canto III, lines 105–10, the preparation of coffee is treated with equal ceremony, elaborate and costly paraphernalia are used, divine 'Spirits' blaze an answer when the 'silver Lamp' is raised in supplication; the liquids flow 'gratefully', inundating '*China*'s Earth' as if in response to prayer. The picture created is that of the Yang-tse-kiang in full flood, but Pope is merely describing the pouring of coffee into fragile china cups – a use of periphrasis on a magnificent scale that, like the toilette sequence and the 'damnation' of the erring sylphs, emphasises the way in which the rituals of social triviality and personal vanity have replaced the more important and valuable rituals of prayer, spiritual activity and meditation in women's everyday lives.

We have seen how Pope draws upon a variety of inherited sources, some but not all of them literary, in order to write his mock-heroic poem. But his 'mockery' is not directed at the classical poem he imitates: it ridicules instead the elegant society which is his subject and his theme. The several elements of language, metaphor, association, image, allusion and rhythmic movement function separately and in judicious combination to create a picture of a young woman of great personal charm moving in a society of remarkable brilliance – yet the perfection of each is spoiled by wrongly focused moral standards. The function of Pope's satire is to help Belinda and her world to a better balanced perspective, on life and on themselves; and since at least part of the process of reform must include the fostering of good sense and 'good Humour', the classic intention of the satirist to aim at reform through laughter is admirably fulfilled by Pope's attitude to his subject and the various devices he employs in writing his poem. Belinda's 'world' glitters in Pope's presentation, it sparkles with beauty, talent, wealth and wit, albeit misused. Just beneath this attractive surface, however, lurk corruption and unpleasantness: for just as Belinda's day of conquests and coquettishness begins, the Courts of Justice close:

> The hungry Judges soon the Sentence sign,   III, 21
> And Wretches hang that Jury-men may dine.

At Hampton Court, the scene of Belinda's countless triumphs, we see British statesmen speculate on the staying-power of certain feminine reputations (III, 6). These are indications that Belinda's 'world' is only a very small part of the real world. Further hints indicate that a good proportion of the apparent realities of Belinda's world are shadowy, even non-existent: Clarissa warns that beauty passes, that only good humour and virtue are real and lasting. This is a flat contradiction of the scheme of values according to which Belinda's world functions, and so it is ignored: but it is the core of the poem's message.

Pope's own position in relation to the poem is that of a man at home in the society he describes, sensuously responsive to its attractions yet sensitive to its follies and corruption. His avowed intention in writing it was merely to laugh two quarrelling families together again by wittily exposing the confused values, arrogance and vanity that had driven them asunder in the first place. But already we see here the beginnings of a deeper interest, the moral analysis of a social environment, and a craftsman's intentness on shaping even the smallest object that passes through his hands into a work of art.

4

'The varying verse, the full-resounding line'

In *An Essay on Criticism* Pope discusses the management and judgment of the heroic couplet as if it were the only known poetic form. As a writer of pastorals, admirer of Milton, and future editor of Shakespeare, Pope knew the other metres and forms of English verse; but his warnings against permitting harmony to prevail over sense, against the tedium of 'equal syllables', repeated rhymes, and irrelevant use of special effects such as the 'Alexandrine', are all applicable to couplet verse more than to any other forms of writing. This, and his assigning to Dryden the pre-eminence Timotheus had formerly enjoyed (lines 382–3), are instances of the 'Augustan' superciliousness, the open assumption of a conscious superiority that was to irritate later poets of different interests and convictions such as Keats, who charged that Pope and his followers had merely

> taught a school
> Of dolts to smooth, inlay, and clip, and fit,
> Till, like the certain wands of Jacob's wit
> Their verses tallied. Easy was the task:
> A thousand handicraftsmen wore the mask
> Of Poesy.

To Keats, the writers of couplet verse were men who had lost touch with the true meaning and glory of poetry –

> with a puling infant's force
> They swayed about upon a rocking-horse
> And thought it Pegasus.

The heroic couplet is, in effect, the sister-metre of blank verse, both forms using a like number of beats to a line (five) and a like number of syllables (ten). Their difference lies in the fact that the unrhymed lines of blank verse permit the poet to follow his thought from one line to the next and beyond if he wishes to do so, using the rule regarding the number of syllables and beats (or 'feet') to help him vary and check his progress. The dramatic

48

possibilities of such a scheme were well understood by Shakespeare, whose skilful use of the metre in passages of human and dramatic conflict creates an artistic approximation to life:

> O that this too, too solid flesh would melt,
> Thaw and resolve itself into a dew
> Or that the everlasting had not fixed
> His canon 'gainst self-slaughter. God, God,
> How weary, stale, flat and unprofitable
> Seem to me all the uses of this world . . .

These lines fall on our ear with the naturalness of deeply-felt *speech*, but they are in fact organised and artistically heightened by the existence of an unperceived skeletal 'scaffolding' upon which they have been arranged. We know the metrical scaffolding is there, not because it calls our attention to itself, but because we hear Hamlet's despairing words beating, as it were, against it. To one of Pope's 'tuneful Fools' who wished only to please his ear with smooth harmony, Shakespeare's lines would have seemed rough and uneven, with a superabundance of syllables, as in line 5; line 4 being, on the other hand, a syllable short. The actor who speaks these lines would regard the pause after the first 'God!' as invaluable, a stage-direction that speaks for itself; but to the reader in his study who expects a syllable to chime in at that point and is bewildered by the 'empty' space, the effect seems all wrong.

The heroic couplet aimed at doing very different things. Shakespeare had used it occasionally himself, to give a scene a neat finish; and this quality of neatness, finality and decorum is the key to its special character. While Shakespeare explored human feeling in blank verse paragraphs, Dryden found the couplet the perfect medium for political satire and argument: modes demanding writing that was reasonable rather than exploratory, ratiocinative rather than imaginative. The apparent irregularity of the blank verse line lends itself to meditative or dramatic expression of a personal kind: we seem to overhear Hamlet's thoughts. The regularity of rhymed couplet verse, on the other hand, seems to presuppose the presence of a genial, contemporary listener to whom the poet addresses himself. The difference that strikes us most forcibly between the passage from *Hamlet* quoted above and the passage from Dryden's *Mac Flecknoe* that follows, is a difference of tone –

All human things are subject to decay
And, when Fate summons, monarchs must obey.
This Flecknoe found, who, like Augustus, young
Was called to empire, and had governed long,
In prose and verse was owned without dispute
Through all the realms of Nonsense, absolute.
This aged prince, now flourishing in peace
And blest with issue of a large increase,
Worn out with business, did at length debate
To settle the succession of the state;
And pondering which of all his sons was fit
To reign and wage immortal war with wit.
Cried, ''Tis resolved, for Nature pleads that he
Should only rule who most resembles me.
Shadwell alone my perfect image bears,
Mature in dulness from his tender years;
Shadwell alone of all my sons is he,
Who stands confirmed in full stupidity.
The rest to some faint meaning make pretence,
But Shadwell never deviates into sense.
Some beams of wit on other souls may fall,
Strike through and make a lucid interval;
But Shadwell's genuine night admits no ray,
His rising fogs prevail upon the day. . .'

Here Dryden describes the preparations made by a king (of
letters) to abdicate his throne in favour of his favourite son. His
tone is elevated, as is appropriate to such a subject. 'All human
things are subject to decay' is the kind of sententious truism with
which politicians' speeches give notice that change is contem-
plated. The statement has, moreover, a sweeping grandeur of
general application that affects us: we feel our own experience
included in it, and we feel ourselves to be listeners as the abdi-
cation is being planned for our benefit (while Hamlet in his soli-
loquy excluded us, his communion being with God and his own
conscience). The first 5 lines of Dryden's poem sustain this grandeur of tone. The flourishes convince, the comparisons of Flecknoe to the youthful Emperor Augustus seem fitting – until line 6,
with its interjection of the single word 'Nonsense', which renders
worthless all that has gone before. Flecknoe reigns supreme, but
his realm is a contemptible one. The attack derives its sting from
the rising tone of adulation and from the impressive diction
employed to build up an impression of Flecknoe's might; its effectiveness from the rhythmic skill that permits no pause at the end

of line 3 and only a very slight one at the end of line 4. The reader who finds the sense of the passage running on from line to line is very ready to rest at the end of the next couplet: he goes full pelt for the last word, but just before he reaches it there, in his path, is the word 'Nonsense', gaining emphasis from its climactic position in the passage and also from its sheer unexpectedness. From now on, Dryden releases shaft after shaft of insult in tones of ecstatic praise, so that his satire gains power from the tension generated between what is actually being said, and the contradictory manner adopted for saying it. Sometimes this is done with a single word – in line 12 it is the word 'wit', in line 16 it is 'dulness', in line 18 it is 'stupidity', in line 23 it is 'night', in line 24 it is 'fogs' – depending for effect upon a reversal of the reader's expectations. Since Flecknoe is nominating Dryden's enemy Shadwell for the Throne of Dulness, all Shadwell's literary activities are fulsomely praised by Dryden as glorious victories won in the course of a life-long struggle with wit, intelligence, reason, truth, sense and morality. Remembering Pope's readiness in *An Essay on Criticism* to

> praise the *Easie Vigor* of a Line,   360
> Where *Denham's* Strength, and *Waller's* Sweetness join

we could find 'strength' and 'vigor' in the fertility of Dryden's invention, idea following idea in quick succession, each one fully and firmly grasped, and satisfactorily followed through. But there is 'sweetness' too, in the harmonious management of the verse, which gives an impression of flowing with the utmost ease; in the air of open-eyed wonder with which he affects to praise Flecknoe and his crew of literary mediocrities; and in the saccharine flattery that coats the insults he directs at them. Yet there is no sense of strain, all is in harmony.

This verse is what it is, largely because it is written in the couplet form. The paired lines encourage an epigrammatic style of expression, the end-rhymes lending additional emphasis to keywords such as 'absolute' in line 6 and 'stupidity' in line 18. The easy, almost casual tone removes all hint of personal animus from the verse, and turns all to laughter. So successfully is personal feeling excluded from the poem that Dryden might almost have been writing to amuse himself. But he entertains us too, and in such a way that we can never, after reading his poem, take

Flecknoe, Shadwell and their kind seriously again. The passage is, in fact, an apt illustration of Dryden's own remarks on true Satire, which at its best should execute its victim with so precise a stroke that his head remains steady on his shoulders. The delicate exactness of Dryden's satiric stroke is made possible by his refining of the rhyming couplet into a weapon flexible enough for his purpose. Given added power by his use of it in stage drama, and the writing of religious and political pamphlets, the couplet developed in Dryden's hands into a medium especially fitted for argument, conversation, and witty, searching comment on the contemporary scene. In this form it descended to Pope.

Pope gave early demonstration in *An Essay on Criticism* (see Chapter 2, pp. 28–9) that he was aware of the couplet's musical possibilities and knew how to use them. He fully understood the art of making sound echo and enact the sense of his verse, just as he was familiar with the stock diction weaker poets relied upon to fulfil the demands made on them by this difficult measure. Where so many rhymes were called for, where a line had to be provided with its requisite number of ten syllables and five iambic 'feet', poets were often pushed to the point of using clichés: hence the gentle fun Pope makes of the 'cooling Western Breeze' that so inevitably 'whispers thro' the Trees' in the verse of other men. The formality forced upon most poets by the regularity of the metre made periphrasis necessary: for where a poet's tone is elevated and formal, ordinary things cannot be mentioned ordinarily without running the risk of anticlimax, incongruity, and even of bathos. And so in the work of many eighteenth-century writers, ordinary things were made to look – and sound – as impressive as possible, to be in keeping with a poet's elevated tone: fish swimming in a stream could become 'purple Warriors of a Tyrian Dye', an arrow could become 'a feather'd Death', birds were members of 'the Airy Race'. Such terms of reference were related to the contemporary tendency to see the created Universe as stratified, divided up into 'races', categories, 'genres' of various kinds; but periphrasis too often leads to the fault of pompous banality. At its worst it was the source of the 'gaudy diction' that Wordsworth in later years was to censure so strongly. But Pope himself was not – at any rate in his mature poetry – often guilty of it. His work affords thousands of examples of ways in which the couplet's many possibilities are fully explored, developed and extended. His objective seems to have consistently been 'correct-ness', that union of strength of mind with sweetness of versifica-tion that he saw exemplified in the poetry of Dryden: and his rule the insistence upon 'varied' and alternating effects expressed in *An Essay on Criticism* (lines 374–83).

While we should probably be right to view Pope's *Pastorals*, *Windsor Forest*, *Eloisa to Abelard* and the *Elegy to the Memory of an Unfortunate Lady* as being largely experiments and tech-nical exercises, they have in common an element of emotional feeling – what his age called 'sentiment', and a later one was to call 'sensibility' – that is conspicuously absent in his later and most mature poetry. Feeling is present in his *Epistles* and *Imita-tions of Horace*, but it is altogether of another kind and linked to general interest and public occasions. In the poems we are about to examine, however, Pope's starting-point seems to be a tender affection for a place, a person (real, imaginary, or histori-cally celebrated like Heloise), or a personal ideal. A good deal of the young poet's technical experiments concern themselves with fitting the heroic couplet to this kind of theme and interest. And since in the processes of such experiment a serious poet develops with his medium, each yielding something to the other, the history of Pope's development as a poet could be regarded on one level as a history of transactions between a writer and his medium.

The first part of *Windsor Forest* (1713) was written contem-poraneously with the *Pastorals*, and employed the pastoral mode to describe the familiar landscape of the district in which Pope had spent part of his childhood and early youth. Having formally invited the Muses and wood-nymphs to bless the poem and aid the poet, Pope goes on to compare the Forest to the Garden of Eden (lines 7–10), and discovers in its orderly beauty a harmoni-ous society characteristic of Nature herself:

> Not *Chaos*-like together crush'd and bruis'd,   13
> But as the World, harmoniously confus'd:
> Where Order in Variety we see,
> And where, tho' all things differ, all agree.

The lines reflect Pope's belief (see Chapter 1: Introductory) in the 'reasonable' philosophical theories current in his time regard-ing the nature of the universe, and illustrate his expectation and desire that his own environment should reflect 'natural' order and harmony. In the lines that follow –

> Here waving Groves a checquer'd Scene display,   17
> And part admit and part exclude the Day;
> As some coy Nymph her Lover's warm Address
> Nor quite indulges, nor can quite repress

Pope displays skill in making sound and rhythm enact meaning, for the placing of the pause in line 18 after 'admit' seems itself to separate shade and sunshine, neatly dividing the verse-line –

> And part admit / and part exclude the Day

an effect repeated in the line that illustrates his statement –

> Nor quite indulges, / nor can quite repress.

The lines recall Milton's rustics dancing 'in the checkered shade', and like so many of Pope's pastoral pieces bear early evidence of the Miltonic influence that exists in his work as a minor strain and was to be passed on through him to Gray, Collins and James Thomson, becoming by this process an important strand of pre-Romanticism in English poetry. We recognise also the beginnings here of the easy, conversational tone that was to become characteristic of Pope; the pauses in lines 18 and 20 are of the kind natural to easy, rational conversation – partly this, partly that', one might say, or 'On the one hand . . . / on the other . . .' – there being implied always a possible alternative. The final couplet, which likens the grove to 'a coy Nymph', carries overtones of sophisticated coquettishness in the word 'coy' that reflect the world of urban gallantry rather than that of Arcadia; and in that world conversation was a civilised pleasure, and cultivated as an art.

> See! from the Brake the whirring Pheasant springs,   111
> And mounts exulting on triumphant Wings;
> Short is his Joy! he feels the fiery Wound,
> Flutters in Blood, and panting beats the Ground.
> Ah! what avail his glossie, varying Dyes,
> His Purple Crest, and Scarlet-circled Eyes,
> The vivid Green his shining Plumes unfold;
> His painted Wings, and Breast that flames with Gold?

The bird's bright, glowing colouring, described with a painter's interest and exactness, contributes brilliance to the total picture. A somewhat similar treatment of fish repeats this effect:

Our plenteous Streams a various Race supply;   141
The bright-ey'd Perch with Fins of *Tyrian* Dye,
The silver Eel, in shining Volumes roll'd,
The yellow Carp, in Scales bedrop'd with Gold,
Swift Trouts, diversify'd with Crimson Stains,
And Pykes, the Tyrants of the watry Plains.

Pope's concern in both passages is, at least partly, with precise description. The pheasant's flight and fall make a familiar, even somewhat obvious moral point, but the energy of the passage lies in the skilful management of a versification that imitates the bird's surging flight and abrupt end. In the second passage, however, even as we admire the virtuosity displayed in the varied treatment of eel and carp, we might well ask why mere fish are elevated in a serious poem to such heights of 'heroic' grandeur: pike seen as warriors in their liquid element, and perch presented as possessing fins of '*Tyrian* Dye'? Does the poem gain anything from such an involved, roundabout way of describing the insignificant?

When we ask these questions, we are reacting with impatience to a certain elaborateness of diction that we might allow to pass if it had been used of objects we could regard as grand enough to justify it. Such grandeur seems wasted on mere fish – destined (as this very verse-paragraph makes clear) in any case for no more heroic fate than the dinner-table of the 'patient Fisher'. In responding in this manner we would not only be making a relevant and justified criticism of periphrasis in poetry, but we would be judging Pope's poem according to his own rule (see *An Essay on Criticism*, lines 243–52, and Chapter 2, p. 30) that a work of art should appeal as a whole and not only or chiefly by the virtue of particular parts. The grandeur of style that is appropriate to certain parts of *Windsor Forest* (see lines 397—422, for example) does not seem to suit other parts quite as well, and this incongruity prevents the poem's various elements coming '*united* to th'admiring *Eyes*'.

A young poet's inability, at this stage of his development, to master completely the difficult art of making easy transitions from one theme of his poem to others is chiefly responsible for the woodenness of *Windsor Forest*, especially when we contrast it with the skilled modulations of Pope's mature poetry. The rhymes that end each pair of lines and the metre's formal regularity are

features of the heroic couplet that impose a tendency to formality
on the poet who uses it. A certain elevation of tone is forced
upon him by the fact that the emphatic effects of rhyme and
regular metre are built into the form, and influence everything
he says in the direction of argument and declamation. If the idea
to be expressed is in any case an elevated one, the poet might
experience little difficulty. But if it is not really thought-pro-
voking, nor even emotionally moving – if, for instance, it is a
mere passing comment on some minor feature of the landscape –
the poet might find himself in real difficulties because the couplet
gives him no relief or respite. He has to go on using it, even in
passages that should be merely transitional, until the next really
profound or moving passage occurs that will give him a chance
to use his medium as it should be used. *Windsor Forest* seems
uneven and unwieldy because all things, large and small, important and trivial, get much the same kind of treatment in it.
Despite its many attractive passages, the poem lacks shapeliness
because its author had not as yet mastered the skill he so much
appreciated in Dryden of making 'varied lays surprise' and bid-
ding 'alternate passions fall and rise'.

In both *Eloisa to Abelard* (1717) and the *Elegy to the Memory
of an Unfortunate Lady* (1717), Pope had well-timed opportu-
nities to concentrate on this particular weakness. In *Eloisa* he set
himself to mirror the movements of a mind ravaged by its efforts
to contain secular and religious feelings of a passionate and
mutually exclusive kind, in the *Elegy* to compose a genre poem
that embodied extremes of feeling and brought them to a satisfactory resolution in the manner of Milton's elegy, *Lycidas*.
Pope's failure in *Windsor Forest* is redeemed in different ways in
the two poems that succeeded it, and each of these seems to stand
as a milestone that marks his progress as a poet. Each put the
couplet to different, difficult uses, each calls for the controlling
power of thought and artistry to operate on feeling of great
intensity.

For the deliberate poet of the eighteenth century, the process
of moulding (into the form required by generic rules material
that had been thrown off in the working out of an original
inspiration) could amount to a secondary process of composition.
Far from being a mechanical 'handicraftsman's task' it was often

in such labour that a poem's artistic integrity was rescued, that the finest effects were achieved (cf. pp. 67–8). *Elegy to the Memory of an Unfortunate Lady* is a poem that seems ready at any moment to split into half a dozen disparate sections were it not for an intelligent artistry that welds them by means of skilfully managed transitional passages into an aesthetically and intellectually satisfactory whole. The original feeling may be modified as a result, but a harmony is achieved: a '*Whole* at once' both '*Bold, and Regular*'. In *Eloisa*, where Pope's subject matter is not of his own invention, the general effect is not quite so tidy, and generic controls do not influence the flow of feeling which, being Eloisa's and not Pope's, it is the couplet's task to reflect rather than to formalise.

In his 'Argument' or preface to *Eloisa*, Pope indicated where his interest lay:

Abelard and *Eloisa* flourish'd in the twelfth Century; they were two of the most distinguish'd persons of their age in learning and beauty, but for nothing more famous than for their unfortunate passion. After a long course of Calamities, they retired each to a several Convent, and consecrated the remainder of their days to religion. It was many years after this separation, that a letter of *Abelard*'s to a Friend which contain'd the history of his misfortune, fell into the hands of *Eloisa*. This awakening all her tenderness, occasion'd those celebrated letters (out of which the following is partly extracted) which gives so lively a picture of the struggles of grace and nature, virtue and passion.

It was presumably these 'struggles' and emotional conflicts that he wished to explore. The letters of Heloise are, in the original and in prose translation, deeply moving in their frank confession of long-cherished affection and remembered passion. When they are compared with Abelard's formal, deeply religious but stern and self-righteous replies; and again with other letters in which Heloise, giving up the idea of reviving their former relationship, devotes herself to ensuring the continuance of their correspondence by setting her former lover and husband the kind of knotty theological problem she knew he must, in his nature, stir himself to consider and solve; the modern reader cannot but share Pope's sympathy and admiration for such strength of mind and feeling, such generosity of character.

Pope chooses to focus upon the earliest part of the correspondence, where the writer's emotion is at its most intense, increased by the shock of discovery and the pain of remembrance. By attempting, not an essay upon it, but a versification of it, he makes clear his intention to capture if he can this very intensity. By using the rhyming couplet for this purpose, he attempts something with built-in difficulties, chief among which is the fact that a medium which had come to him shaped by Dryden for ratiocinative purposes or for political satire – i.e. for poetry of an essentially public nature, committed to the aim of moulding general opinion in certain clearly defined directions – is now to embody the intensely personal, private thoughts of a woman in love, careless at the time of writing where her passions might lead her.

As the poem opens, the scene is set. Secluded in her convent, surrounded by the Miltonic[1] gloom of

> deep solitudes and awful cells,   1
> Where heav'nly-pensive, contemplation dwells,
> And ever-musing melancholy reigns

Eloisa has read Abelard's letter, and been recalled by it to dangerously vivid memories of their earlier relationship – dangerous, because they are potentially destructive of her carefully developed, cool discipline of body and mind:

> What means this tumult in a Vestal's veins?   4
> Why rove my thoughts beyond this last retreat?
> Why feels my heart its long-forgotten heat?

Her self-questioning ends in a conclusion that combines dread with amazement and an unexpected, strange sensation of triumph:

> Yet, yet I love! – From *Abelard* it came,   7
> And *Eloisa* yet must kiss the name.

The word 'must' implies compulsion: Eloisa feels she is no longer responsible for her own actions. But her tone expresses as much pleasure as it does alarm: there is an element of joy in the deliberate abandonment of her (hitherto strictly regulated) personality to emotion. The 'struggle' between the coldness of the solitary cell and the 'heat' of remembered passion moves quickly from the mind to the body, as Abelard's name passes in the second paragraph from the 'close disguise' of Eloisa's heart to the light of open day with the help of her hand, which has chosen – of its

---

[1] This note of gloom was taken up by Gray, Collins and other late-eighteenth-century poets, as the picturesque–romantic.

own volition – to disobey her conscious will and obey instead the promptings of instinctive feeling –

> Oh write it not, my hand – The name appears   13
> Already written – wash it out, my tears!

In paragraph 3 Eloisa concludes that she has not yet, for all her self-discipline, 'forgot herself to stone'; in this she is unlike the lifeless, inert convent she inhabits, whose surroundings have learned to alter their nature, their 'rugged rocks' having become worn by the knees of penitents and their shady, romantic grottoes begun to bristle with thorns.

Since she is still 'herself' the self that once loved and was loved by Abelard, the rest of the poem is presented from the point of view of an emotional woman under psychological stress. As Eloisa echoes the history of their love that Abelard has related in his letter, she adds to it her own anguished comments, interspersed with pleas that their correspondence should be renewed. Her ostensible reason for this request is, that since she can no longer share his love,[2] she may be allowed at least to sympathise with Abelard in his pain and disappointments (lines 41–50). But as Eloisa recalls the past, her emotions take her from generous sympathy to feeling of a more direct and intimate kind, embittered though it is by her awareness of the bodily and spiritual barriers between them:

> Come! with thy looks, thy words, relieve my woe;   119
> Those still at least are left thee to bestow.
> Still on that breast enamour'd let me lie,
> Still drink delicious poison from thy eye,
> Pant on thy lip, and to thy heart be prest;
> Give all thou canst – and let me dream the rest.

The lines wittily re-enact (the wit carrying painful overtones of sexual frustration) Eloisa's earlier experience when, growing in her acquaintance with Abelard, her youthful spiritual idealism had melted into a warm sexuality –

> Back thro' the paths of pleasing sense I ran,   69
> Nor wish'd an Angel whom I lov'd a Man.

[2] Abelard's punishment for his association with Eloisa was castration, so that all her dreams of a physical reunion between them are (and she knows it) mere fancy. The vows of chastity they have severally taken separate them still further.

This second (although physically limited) back-sliding is immediately followed by a return to self-denial and self-chastisement:

> Ah no! instruct me other joys to prize,   125
> With other beauties charm my partial eyes,
> Full in my view set all the bright abode,
> And make my soul quit *Abelard* for God.

For the first time in Pope's poetry, the couplet is being used to embody the wild swing of emotion and passion from one extreme to another. We note too, however, that its built-in formality helps to regulate the wildness and force of that movement.

In the second part of the poem the complexities of Eloisa's character are more fully displayed. Since her earlier argument has been already rendered invalid by her rapid descent (in the very act of making that argument) to an unguarded display of sensuous feeling, she attempts an alternative. If Abelard cannot write to her without endangering her soul, he could at least write to the members of the convent he had founded –

> Ah think at least thy flock deserves thy care,   129
> Plants of thy hand, and children of thy pray'r.
> From the false world in early youth they fled,
> By thee to mountains, wilds, and deserts led.
> You rais'd these hallowed walls; the desert smil'd,
> And Paradise was open'd in the Wild.

This is followed almost immediately by an honest, involuntary retraction. Eloisa rejects the deceptions of this indirect appeal, and makes instead another of a tender, intensely personal kind, reminding Abelard of the complex relationship she bears to him:

> See how the force of others' pray'rs I try,   149
> (Oh pious fraud of am'rous charity!)
> But why should I on others' pray'rs depend?
> Come thou, my father, brother, husband, friend!
> Ah let thy handmaid, sister, daughter, move,
> And, all those tender names in one, thy love!

She follows this with a cry for spiritual help, declaring that as a result of reading his letter, she has lost the ability to draw spiritual serenity from her surroundings. In a picture that recalls Milton's[3] treatment of similar material in his poem *Il Penseroso*, come visions of death and terror –

[3] See note on p. 58.

> But o'er the twilight groves, and dusky caves,　　163
> Long-sounding isles, and intermingled graves,
> Black Melancholy sits, and round her throws
> A death-like silence, and a dread repose:
> Her gloomy presence saddens all the scene,
> Shades ev'ry flow'r, and darkens ev'ry green,
> Deepens the murmur of the falling floods,
> And breathes a browner horror on the woods.

The gloomy allusions to 'Melancholy', 'silence', 'twilight' and 'sadness' do not merely create atmosphere, they link up with the explicit references to 'death', 'graves' and 'horror' to support Eloisa's charge that Abelard's reappearance in her thoughts has brought her from visions of Heaven to the proximity of Hell and of probable damnation. She argues that it is his responsibility to correct this situation by his presence, or by his written words of advice and sympathy. The weight of her spiritual burden is confessed to him in the succeeding paragraphs: torn between her duty to God and her love for Abelard, Eloisa knows herself to be guilty of a damnable hypocrisy in every moment of every day:

> Ah wretch! believ'd the spouse of God in vain,　　177
> Confess'd within the slave of love and man.
> Assist me heav'n! but whence arose that pray'r?
> Sprung it from piety, or from despair?
> Ev'n here, where frozen chastity retires,
> Love finds an altar for forbidden fires.
> I ought to grieve, but cannot what I ought;
> I mourn the lover, not lament the fault;
> I view my crime, but kindle at the view,
> Repent old pleasures, and sollicit new:
> Now turn'd to heav'n, I weep my past offence,
> Now think of thee, and curse my innocence.

The antithetical development that the rhyming couplet (with its paired rhymes and its mid-line pause) tends to promote is employed here to convey the conflict Eloisa experiences, as her thoughts swing between emotional and intellectual points on a well-understood curve of experience. In balancing reason against its opposite, emotion, and using the caesura to help him to do so, is Pope being somewhat too precise? In the careful measure and alliterative play of

> I mourn the *l*over, / not *l*ament the fault

has feeling been dissipated in an excess of craftsmanship, in 'an epigrammatic effect which lessens and falsifies the emotion'?[4] It could have been, had that emotion been of a vaguer kind. But Eloisa is intelligent as well as emotional: she is surprised only by the strength of her own feeling, not by its nature which she knows very well (according to the religious tenets of her age) to be deserving of eternal punishment. With the gulf of Hell yawning before her, there can be no room or time to spare for half-truths and evasions. If devotion to God guarantees Heaven, her passion for Abelard, because it militates against God's supremacy in her mind, is guilty and must guarantee the punishment of Hell. The conflicting positions are perfectly clear to Eloisa, and as she swings between 'grace and nature, virtue and passion' she is swinging between Heaven and eternal damnation. Through his skilful use of the couplet's capabilities to reflect the psychological crisis of Eloisa, Pope extends the possibilities of the form.

From line 207 onward, Pope contrasts in successive paragraphs the undisturbed serenity of the 'blameless Vestal' (sanctified by heavenly grace while alive, and dying in visions of eternal bliss) with Eloisa's erring, 'unholy joy', her secret nightly indulgence of fancy and imagination to create the single pleasure – albeit a 'curst' one – that is left her; and also with Abelard's own 'dead calm of fix'd repose' (line 251). Loss of the power of sexual response has at least yielded him

> A cool suspense from pleasure and from pain   250

but Eloisa's situation is seen as more terrible by these contrasts, for *she* can enjoy neither the quiet of innocence nor the calm of sexual impotence and trembles, instead, on the edge of damnation:

> I waste the Matin lamp in sighs for thee,   267
> Thy image steals between my God and me,
> Thy voice I seem in ev'ry hymn to hear,
> With ev'ry bead I drop too soft a tear.
> When from the Censer clouds of fragrance roll,
> And swelling organs lift the rising soul;
> One thought of thee puts all the pomp to flight,
> Priests, Tapers, Temples, swim before my sight:
> In seas of flame my plunging soul is drown'd,
> While Altars blaze, and Angels tremble round.

The word 'plunging' is a particularly apt choice, perfectly ex-

[4] Edith Sitwell, *Alexander Pope* (1930, 1948) p. 229.

pressing the wild force with which Eloisa hurtles from one emotional attitude to another. The final couplet provides a foretaste
of damnation, as the 'seas of flame' recall the 'lake of fire burning
with brimstone' of the Book of Revelation, xix, 20, and the angels'
'trembling' reflects their response to Eloisa's dangerous spiritual
situation. The terror of damnation is increased by the way certain words remind us continually that Eloisa's faults are but
natural and human: should she, therefore, be damned for them?
'Trembling' reminds us of the preceding passages, which contrasted Eloisa's natural, human agony with the *un*-natural calm of
Abelard and the 'blameless Vestal'. It reflects sensations more
human than superhuman, transmitting the physical response of
human fear and of sexual passion even more vividly than an
imagined angelic dread. Many details of diction and style link
this part of *Eloisa to Abelard* with certain early poems of Pope[5]
and also with the work of the poet's predecessors[6] which have the
effect of expanding ranges of meaning already present.

The confession of her own dangerous guilt leads Eloisa to a
pitiful (because quite fanciful) prayer that Abelard should appear
as the agent of Hell, cancel out their mutual past of 'sorrows ...
tears . . . fruitless penitence and pray'rs' and dare, in reunion
with her, the certain horrors of damnation (lines 281–8). This
'new' attitude of romantic, daring self-abandonment is not wholly
new, since it looks back to Eloisa's half-guilty joy at the poem's
beginning, in being 'forced' to let disciplinary rules slip at last

[5] The atmosphere of splendidly opulent ritual here recalls the toilette
sequence in *The Rape of the Lock*; while the manner in which 'Priests,
Tapers, Temples' swim before Eloisa's eyes at the thought of her lover
recalls the way '*Wounds, Charms,* and *Ardors*' banished the memory of
Belinda's dream and 'Streets, chairs and coxcombs' replaced Teresa
Blount in the poet's imagination in *An Epistle to a Young Lady on her
leaving the Town, after the Coronation*, all three passages concerning
themselves with the accurate description of the way mental impressions
are blurred or replaced.

[6] The 'blazing' Altars, like the 'bright abode' of Heaven, and the likening
of the convent to a 'Paradise being opened in the Wild' reflect back to
Milton's *Paradise Lost* in matters of particular detail as well as of
general impression, in much the same way that the earlier description of
the Convent's rocks and caverns reflected the dark, carefully contrived
gloom of *Il Penseroso*. Milton remains a presence in Pope's poetry to the
very end and through him influences pre-Romantic poetry.

Lines 323–4 (quoted on p. 64) recall Marlowe's *Dr Faustus*, on
whom Helen's kiss conferred the immortality of damnation. Eloisa's
dying kiss will do the same for Abelard.

and give herself up to the promptings of her heart. But it is not
an attitude that she allows herself to indulge very long. Soon the
swing begins in the opposite direction –

> No, fly me, fly me! far as Pole from Pole;   289
> Rise *Alps* between us! and whole oceans roll!
> Ah come not, write not, think not once of me,
> Nor share one pang of all I felt for thee.
> Thy oaths I quit, thy memory resign,
> Forget, renounce me, hate whate'er was mine.

This attitude is quite as fanciful as the last. Abelard remaining as
a result of his physical condition quite unmoved by all her
appeals, there can be as far as he is concerned nothing to 'forget'
or 'renounce'. She is indulging a final self-deception, and after
this there is nothing left but withdrawal from passion to resignation. Eloisa will return to her spiritual disciplines. As she con-
templates her own death, Abelard reappears in conflicting visions.
But the erotic picture of a lover who will

> See my lips tremble, and my eye-balls roll,   323
> Suck my last breath, and catch my flying soul!

changes to that of the prelate who will

> Present the Cross before my lifted eye,   327
> Teach me at once, and learn of me to die.

It is interesting to note that Eloisa writes her own 'epitaph':
having pictured her own death and Abelard's performance of the
last rites, she projects his own eventual death watched by Angels
and embraced by Saints (lines 337–42), and imagines two lovers
weeping in aftertimes over their shared tomb:

> O'er the pale marble shall they join their heads,   349
> And drink the falling tears each other sheds,
> Then sadly say, with mutual pity mov'd,
> Oh may we never love as these have lov'd!

It would seem that when Pope indulged himself in feeling and
sentiment – especially of a pathetic kind – his saving wit was
capable (like that of certain later Metaphysical poets such as
Crashaw and Cowley) of partial or temporary flight. The baroque,
indeed faintly comic, picture of the lovers drinking each other's
tears gives a work of quite considerable achievement an unfortunate end. Eloisa's invocation of 'some future Bard' who would

experience sorrow similar to her own (lines 359–64) introduces another false note: she has begun to dramatise (and therefore to enjoy) her self-pity. The last couplet, picturing her 'pensive ghost' retaining literary judgment to such a degree that its sorrows might be soothed by a poet's skilful singing of her 'woes' gives the poem a neat end, but it undermines the impression of an intelligent and passionate femininity, of a conflict between 'grace and nature' fully grasped and painfully experienced, that Pope responded to in the original letters of Heloise and succeeds – in the greater part of his poem – in capturing and recreating.

5

'. . . And energy divine'

The Augustan Age, eminently an Age of Reason and one sus-
picious of emotionalism, did not produce many serious elegies,
preferring to dignify death by means of the epitaph, a mode of
writing – like the elegy – that took the form of a solemn lament,
but one brief enough to read as if it had been designed for inscrip-
tion on a monument or a gravestone. Mock-elegies, of course,
abounded. These provided plenty of scope for wit, and were an
effective means of attack or exposure through contrast of 'low' or
ludicrous subject mater with a high and solemn rhetorical manner. Pope lived in an age in which early death and incurable
disease were facts of contemporary living one had to come to
terms with. Reason and good sense did not favour a melancholy
or nostalgic lingering on the morbid subjects of death and loss,
unless it took the brief, decent and appropriate form of the epitaph – which had the added advantage of seeming to possess a
social function and not to exist simply as an excuse for emotional
self-indulgence.

We have seen from our reading of *Eloisa to Abelard*, however,
that Pope possessed a capacity for intense feeling. It never left
him, and he retained to the end of his life a spontaneous respon-
siveness to a pathetic subject or situation. 'Tenderness', he wrote
in a letter to Lady Mary Wortley Montagu in 1718, 'is the very
emanation of good sense and virtue; the finest minds, like the
finest metals, dissolve the easiest.' His *Epistle to Augustus* (1737)
carries an expression of lonely affection for the sentiment in
Cowley's poetry:

> Who now reads Cowley? if he pleases yet,   75
> His moral pleases, not his pointed wit,
> Forgot his Epic, nay Pindaric Art,
> But still I love the language of his Heart.

Death has always been, and will always be a theme that tempts
the poet who chooses to write upon it into traps of sentimentality

and emotionalism. Pope was no exception: in writing his *Elegy to the Memory of an Unfortunate Lady* he exposed his art to the dangers inherent for all poets in such themes as this poem focuses upon – heroic individualism victimised by calculating reason; sudden and tragic death. The success of the poem is hard-won, and of a precarious kind. It is perhaps significant that Pope did not attempt the elegiac form again.

The weapons with which the Age of Reason fended off emotionalism were Wit and good (or common) Sense. An ability to control emotion by subjecting it to witty reasoning can be seen in the epitaphs Pope composed: *On Sir William Trumbull* (1716), for example, *On Edmund Duke of Buckingham* (1736), or *On Mrs Corbet, Who dyed of a Cancer in her Breast* (1730) in which death – even of the most painful kind – provides him with occasion for the kind of levity that relieves the feelings by contrasting with (and thereby often focusing more clearly) the reason for sorrow. The presence of such wit in Pope's serious poetry indicates, as F. R. Leavis has observed (endorsing Middleton Murry's recognition of its 'Metaphysical' elements), that 'Pope is as much the last poet of the seventeenth century as the first of the eighteenth'.[1] But 'wit' in Pope's poetry includes also that other aspect of an Augustan poet's artistic sense, the shaping intelligence that makes of re-writing and 'polishing' another stage of composition (see Chapter 4, pp. 56–7). It includes the sense of tradition that is strong in a generic poet aware of his predecessors' achievements in the mode he wishes to essay. Above all, it exists there as a feeling for skill and grace that holds Pope steady above the extremes of feeling, a trapeze that enables his art to swing with breath-taking precision between them, making beauty out of every twist and perilous turn. There are times when the reader of the *Elegy* catches his breath: will the poet fall this time? will he slip into sentimentality? into anger? into hatred? A sense of being precariously poised never leaves us as we read this poem.

Some of these aspects of Pope's 'wit' merit closer consideration before we turn to the poem. It is important to keep in mind, for instance, the fact that the impression the *Elegy* gives of emotional spontaneity and lifelike contradictoriness is most certainly the result of art. In its first four verse paragraphs we are made aware of a current of wildly swinging, emotional feeling. Lines 1–5

[1] F. R. Leavis, 'Pope', *Revaluation* (1935).

initiate an atmosphere of theatrical melodrama, with their 'moon-light shade' and the appearance of a 'beck'ning ghost' complete with 'visionary' weapon as in Shakespeare's *Macbeth* or *Hamlet*; lines 6–10 switch abruptly to a passionate justification of love that is uncontrolled by wisdom or prudence –

Is it, in heav'n, a crime to love too well?   6

This is followed by a condemnation of ordinary humankind as a race of inferior dullards (lines 17–24); and another sudden change in the poem's tone has the 'speaker' calling down the vengeance of heaven upon certain wicked and unfeeling persons (lines 35–42). The reader is intended to regard these changes of tone as the natural expression of a man in the grip of spontaneous emotion, who swings from one extreme of feeling to another: this response is carefully induced and deliberately calculated for. The impression the poem gives of emotional spontaneity is belied, however, not only by the strict attention to technical matters required by Pope's superlative control of his metre, but by the very deliberate structuring we perceive if we examine the *Elegy*'s argument closely. Three paragraphs present a point of view and raise several issues that demand consideration, a fourth brings these issues into forceful collision, and three more lead away once again in the direction of a satisfactory and peaceful conclusion. Although in its final form the transitional passages that blend one idea into the next and relate all parts to the whole artfully combine to convey an impression of naturalness, it would be naive and unrealistic on our part to think of this poem as having been 'spontaneously' composed. Part of the process of composition for the *Elegy* (as for all Pope's poetry) would have been the act of shaping, of pulling together, of making deliberate choices with regard to lines to be omitted, lines to be included, lines to be freshly written, lines to be polished up. The personal experience in which the poem originated would have had to be brought into line with what was generally expected of the elegiac form, in-herited and contemporary; and this consideration would have affected not only the mood of the poem, but its structure and organisation.

In writing his *Elegy*, this most traditional of poets had at least two models before him: the elegy of Roman classical tradition, and the example of Milton. In many technical details Pope's

Elegy approximates to the Roman pattern: a line such as 64 – '(Let) the green turf lie lightly on thy breast' – looks back to the *Sit tibi terra levis* so common on Roman gravestones that it was often abbreviated to S.T.T.L. The unhappy suicide who is the subject of the poem is presented as a person of finer moral fibre than most people:

> Why bade ye else, ye Pow'rs! her soul aspire   11
> Above the vulgar flight of low desire?
> Ambition first sprung from your blest abodes;
> The glorious fault of Angels and of Gods:
> Thence to their Images on earth it flows,
> And in the breasts of Kings and Heroes glows!

The honourable self-murder that was a 'Roman's part' is considered by the speaker to add to the Lady's nobility of character, and Pope's use of the form, together with his allusion to 'Heroes' and 'Kings', reminds the reader that there are standards other than the Christian, according to which the Lady's death would be thought noble, inevitable, even admirable. The 'Pow'rs' of heaven are closer to the Olympians than to a Christian divinity; 'Gods' suggests them too, recalling Titanic battles in the universe and such incidents from classical myth as Phaeton's ambition to drive the chariot of the Sun. There must be an appropriate reward for the Lady in heaven, the poet seems to assert, for why else would the 'Pow'rs' of heaven prompt her to seek it through suicide? Where Christian doctrine protests against such an assertion, the poet builds up a case for the Lady, supporting it by the allusion to the 'blest abodes' of the classical epic and by the details we have just considered that recall the classical tradition. We should note before leaving the subject, however, that certain parts of the poem seem to belong to a Christian context: the allusion to 'Angels' in line 14 (presumably Satan's squadron) is one of these, and the Lady's terrifying appearance as a restless, wandering spirit shut out of a Christian heaven is another.

The co-existence in the *Elegy* of Christian and classical elements recalls Pope's other model, Milton's elegy to his friend Edward King, *Lycidas*. But there are many other correspondences. Milton's greater work stands in the background of Pope's *Elegy*. Less a lament for personal loss than a meditation on the way fate seems to frustrate the aims of serious and dedicated poets, *Lycidas* leaves its mark on Pope's poem which, in turn, extends beyond the

limited purpose of a lament for the death of a real or imaginary
'Lady' to consider the part played by deep and intense feeling
in the human (and especially poetic) personality. The Miltonic
legacy is apparent in more particular ways as well, notably in
lines 49–68 of the *Elegy*, where a shift of tone from fury to calm
is managed by Pope in a manner unmistakably learned from
Milton's resolution of a somewhat similar problem in *Lycidas*.
Milton introduces a fierce St Peter into a pagan, pastoral poem
and nearly shatters its fragile structure by doing so. Peace is
restored with a call to the river-God Alpheus to return –

> – the dread voice is past
> That shrunk thy streams –

and this is followed by the return also of the 'Sicilian Muse'
with a graceful 'flower' passage in the course of which St Peter's
fiery denunciations are allowed to fade from the reader's memory.
The parallel begins in Pope's *Elegy* with line 35:

> Thus, if eternal justice rules the ball,
> Thus shall your wives, and thus your children fall:
> On all the line a sudden vengeance waits,
> And frequent hearses shall besiege your gates.
> There passengers shall stand, and pointing say,
> (While the long fun'rals blacken all the way)
> Lo these were they, whose souls the Furies steel'd,
> And curs'd with hearts unknowing how to yield.

An Old Testament fury rages blackly through the passage, the
implacable demand for 'an eye for an eye, a tooth for a tooth'
that we associate with the Jewish prophets of old (or, appropriately to a 'Roman' elegy, with classical ideas of vengeance and
honour). The besieging hearses and long, black lines of funeral
coaches vividly emphasise the force of this denunciation of the
Lady's false kin, which is modified by no saving grace of Christ-
like mercy or compassion. The fall of the Lady's tormentors is
seen as logical, inevitable according to the moral law the speaker
assumes to rule the universe, and fully deserved –

> So perish all, whose breast ne'er learn'd to glow   45
> For others' good, or melt at others' woe.

The alliteration and balance in the lines that follow will suggest
to the reader who has appreciated the function of these devices

in *The Rape of the Lock* or *An Essay on Criticism*, that a
sense of proportion is returning to the poet as well as to the
poem:

> What can atone (oh ever-injur'd shade!)   47
> Thy fate un*p*ity'd, / and thy rites un*p*aid?

And he will be right, for the next lines produce a significant
change in tone:

> No friend's complaint, no kind domestic tear   49
> Pleas'd thy pale ghost, or grac'd thy mournful bier;
> By foreign hands thy dying eyes were clos'd,
> By foreign hands thy decent limbs compos'd,
> By foreign hands thy humble grave adorn'd,
> By strangers honour'd, and by strangers mourn'd!

Doubly welcome after the angry denunciation that has just ended,
is this formal patterning of words and phrases that indicate the
unobtrusive entry into the poem of a concern for form and shapeliness. Pope's picture of the Lady, now arranged after her death
for burial, is appropriately formal, itself an 'arrangement'. From
this point the poem progresses to a lyrical evocation of the natural
beauty of the Lady's grave. She has been excluded by reason of
her suicide from the grace of burial in hallowed ground, but the
true worth of her character sanctifies (significantly aided by
Nature itself) the ordinary earth in which she lies:

> Yet shall thy grave with rising flow'rs be drest,   63
> And the green turf lie lightly on thy breast:
> There shall the morn her earliest tears bestow,
> There the first roses of the year shall blow;
> While Angels with their silver wings o'ershade
> The ground, now sacred by thy reliques made.

The 'natural' mourning that Nature yields the Lady, in the form
of 'tears' of dew, the 'roses' of springtime, the pall of living,
'rising flow'rs' that will 'dress' her grave, is at once more permanent (being renewable with the changes of the year) and more
valuable than the indecorous artificialities and 'mockery of woe'
that the Lady's fashionable 'friends in sable weeds' (lines 56–8)
could have offered her. The word 'reliques' suggests that the
Lady is herself holy, a saint deserving the care of silver-winged
angels. Pope's skilful management of such a transition as this from
energetic rage to quietness and calm owes a good deal to *Lycidas*,

as a careful examination of the parallel passages will reveal. It is important to recognise that this sense of peaceful resolution on which the *Elegy* ends has been achieved by the recollection of Milton's example, the sense of being part of a literary tradition, and the techniques of deliberate craftsmanship.

In our discussion of the poem so far it has emerged that two opposing 'passions' appear to struggle for mastery over the speaker's mind: love of the Lady for whose character and pre-dicament he feels a spiritual affinity, and resentment (rising to hatred) of her unfeeling relatives. In his treatment of the two, Pope alternates wit with sentiment until he brings about a variety of poetic polarisation, the relatives being consistently discussed in terms of a closely reasoned, 'Metaphysical' logic, while the Lady is treated exclusively in melodramatic or sentimental terms. This division between subjects and styles begins early in the *Elegy*, with the appearance of the ghostly Lady, 'ever beauteous, ever friendly' (in lines 1–5), in an atmosphere of mystery and uncer-tainty flavoured with a macabre tincture of horror at visual and suspected violence: for 'gor'd' means bloodstained as well as pierced. The reader's sympathy is demanded by the poet for his unhappy heroine, to whom heaven in its cruelty has failed to grant a 'bright reversion' of her fate on earth (lines 9–10). This is followed by a condemnation of the human race in general: the Lady's 'brave' death ('brave' meaning not only courageous, but also beautiful, glorious, heroic) places her in a class apart from and above them:

> Most souls, 'tis true, but peep out once an age,　　　　17
> Dull sullen pris'ners in the body's cage:
> Dim lights of life that burn a length of years,
> Useless, unseen, as lamps in sepulchres;
> Like Eastern Kings a lazy state they keep,
> And close confin'd to their own palace sleep.

The metaphors Pope uses to describe mankind and extends to include the Lady's family are not only effective in the Meta-physical manner of alerting us to new significance by the drawing of unusual analogies, but closely reasoned. The word 'peep' is appropriate, both to the souls seen as 'prisoners' of living bodies, and to their reappearance in the third couplet as oriental poten-tates slumbering in their palaces. The enclosing body might be a mansion, but it is also a prison, for the soul within never achieves more than a glimpse of real, passionate life. The wavering, uncertain rhythm of

> Useless, unseen, as lamps in *sepulchres*

suggests that the mere flicker of emotion of which such souls might be capable is related more to death than to life. We might notice that the poem has swung from an emotional, largely unreasoned and unreasonable justification of the Lady's sensibility to a closely reasoned, logical condemnation of her family's emotional sterility. It seems that the two subjects are so violently opposed to one another that they can be dealt with only separately, and by using different techniques.

This poetic – and emotional – situation is sustained by a remarkable play of Pope's characteristic wit. We have noted (p. 72) that wit seems to alternate with sentiment and melodrama in the *Elegy*, reinforcing the opposition between its subjects. When the speaker reflects on the injustice suffered by the Lady, wit appears to desert the poem, and we are back with the angry gestures of melodrama:

> But thou, false guardian of a charge too good,   29
> Thou, mean deserter of thy brother's blood!
> See on these ruby lips the trembling breath,
> These cheeks, now fading at the blast of death:
> Cold is the breast which warm'd the world before,
> And those love-darting eyes must roll no more.

In the 'false guardian' we have the villain of the piece, who must remain unredeemed by any saving moral virtue, for is not his victim 'too good'? It is she whose blasted youth and beauty plead for our sympathy, and four lines describe her in death so that we may not withhold it. But the quality of feeling in those four lines seems so exaggerated that it would hardly surprise us to come across them in *The Rape of the Lock*. In the ironic comedy of that poem, Belinda needed but to smile 'and all the World was gay'; a touch of chagrin in her could give 'half the World the Spleen'.[2] Yet in the *Elegy* the Lady's breast 'warms the world', and the exaggerated phrase is meant in perfect seriousness. In *The Rape of the Lock* Belinda was told chidingly that

> Beauties in vain their pretty Eyes may roll   v, 33

[2] *The Rape of the Lock*, ii, 52; iv, 78.

but in the *Elegy* we are expected to regard a woman possessed of the same 'rolling' eyes as Belinda and other frivolous belles, as perfectly virtuous and morally far above the common run of humankind. When wit returns to the speaker's treatment of the Lady, it is a wit very different from the cold logic that governs his treatment of her kinsmen:

> As into air the purer spirits flow,   25
> And sep'rate from their kindred dregs below;
> So flew the soul to its congenial place,
> Nor left one virtue to redeem her Race.

In using an apt and economical simile drawn from chemistry (the 'purer spirits' separating from their 'dregs') to illustrate and justify his assertion of the Lady's virtue, the speaker's wit seems to follow a Metaphysical bent. But the argument depends on the willingness of the reader's imagination to grasp the metaphor, not on logic.

Do we recognise in the oppositions of the *Elegy* Pope's personal expression of the conflict that troubled the thinking of the Augustan Age, between Reason on one side and Feeling on the other, between Sense and Sensibility? If this is true, the poem is not only a memorial and justification of a tragic suicide, but would seem to defend Feeling itself, together with Passion and Individualism, those dangerous evils in the presence of which the Augustans walked so warily. Looking at the *Elegy* in terms of structure and tone we will see, how, seemingly deprived of the disciplinary control of wit, the speaker's presentation of the Lady plunges dangerously towards sentimentality in the first six lines of paragraph 4. Next, writing of her relatives from a point of view apparently devoid of compassion and guided by logic alone, he plunges equally dizzily towards a black, unforgiving hate in the rest of the same paragraph. No reconciliation seems possible between such hostile emotions and styles, whose warfare has been prepared for in the preliminary skirmishes of the opening paragraphs: the signs of exaggeration in paragraph 1, with its melodramatic and rhetorical evocation of the Lady's ghost; the tendency to glorify her unnaturally and by illogical means in paragraph 2; and the meretricious use of a 'metaphysical' analogy to justify her continued idealisation in paragraph 3, followed by the arbitrary division of humankind by the speaker into 'purer spirits' and 'base dregs'. After the pitched battle between logic and sentiment that takes up most of paragraph 4, the feeling of the poem shifts (as we have already noted on pp. 70–2) through formal grace, a reappearance of wit and a quieting and ordering of feeling to create visual beauty in paragraph 5. The method by which conflicting poetic styles are reconciled and ordered by means of their subjection to the elegiac mode is itself symbolic of the conflict and reconciliation between Reason and Feeling that form the poem's core.

The issues raised by Milton in *Lycidas* are resolved by him at the poem's end through a characteristic reliance on Christian faith – 'through the dear might of Him who walked on waves'. The reconciliation of opposites in Pope's *Elegy* is equally characteristic of its author, and is brought about by the operation of wit under the direction of the poetic Muse. We are subtly prepared for it by the careful calming of the poem's tone in imitation of Milton in lines 47–68, and the technical devices used there in which the influence of conscious poetic art is implicit. But although the formalities of paragraph 5 calm the atmosphere of the *Elegy*, they do not resolve the conflicts set up earlier. A resolution must be provided in paragraph 6 if the poem is to end satisfactorily; and we find it initiated through an assertion of the Lady's spiritual independence of the conventional trappings and splendour associated with 'great' funerals:

> How lov'd, how honour'd once, avails thee not, 71
> To whom related, or by whom begot;

She lacks the gravestone that might have proclaimed the nobility of her birth and character. But she does not need it. The word 'avails' is one on which the paragraph (and the poem as a whole) now begins to turn: in one sense it surveys ground already covered, reiterating the speaker's admiration for the Lady's moral superiority, but in another its leads forward to an idea totally new in the poem:

> A heap of dust alone remains of thee; 73
> 'Tis all thou art, and all the proud shall be!

The Lady has reached a point at which nothing can 'avail' or help her, she is merely 'a heap of dust'. But she is not alone in her fate, for the speaker has been able at last to include her with her false 'Race' in a single line as sharing the ultimate anonymity

of death. Personalities who could never be reconciled in any part
of the poem, whose attitudes seemed to be in eternal opposition,
are now seen as sharing a single fate; and where they have been
hitherto treated of in alternating paragraphs, composed in different poetic styles, they are brought together at last in a single
line of verse. We can see that this is the reconciliation towards
which the poem has been all the time progressing; and the head-
long drive towards emotionalism and the tendency towards cold,
logical intellectualism have been simultaneously reconciled by the
art of composition, creating in the process a work of art.

It is natural that after the emotional and intellectual reconciliation effected in paragraph 6, the poet should proceed to consider
his own future in the light of what he has learned. (We may see
a similar pattern in *Lycidas*, as the shepherd matter-of-factly
rises – his elegy being sung – and departs to new poetic and
spiritual pastures.) Poets must die themselves, like the subjects of
their poems, except that it will be their skills that must dissolve,
not the lips, eyes, cheeks and breast of a beautiful woman:

> Deaf the prais'd ear, and mute the tuneful tongue.   76

A pun on the word 'want' links the Lady, whose death was caused
by her own sensibility but who lost by that death not only the
power of feeling but the consolation of other people's affection,
with the fact that the poet whose sympathy for her affects him as
if it were death itself

> Shall shortly want the gen'rous tear he pays.   78

As thoughts of his own death fill his imagination, the poet recog-
nises his 'ruling passions' to be two: sensibility (the capacity for
intense feeling, of which the Lady has become a symbol in the
poem) and his devotion to the art of Poetry with its strict disciplines and reliance on wit and reason (of which the Muse is his
personal symbol). This recognition has been prepared for by Pope
and paralleled by the reconciliation in line 74 of the Lady with
her proud relations. The terms in which the poet addresses the
twin sources of his inspiration –

> The Muse *forgot*, and thou *belov'd* no more –

suggest that the Muse (daughter as she is, of Memory) inhabits
the world of the mind, while the Lady lives in the instinctive

affections. The linking of the two in the poem's last line symbolises the way the art of composition can reconcile warring elements in literature. The *Elegy* is, in fact, carefully structured to
tell the tale of its own composition, to demonstrate how uncontrolled feeling and cold intellectualism can tear a poem apart
between them unless they are called to order and subjected to the
rules of art. Pope's success in fusing sensibility and wit, in joining
heart and mind, indicates a recognition that real life, like the life
of a poem, can be properly conducted only if both deities control
it in harmony.

The transitional passages that connect each extreme and contradictory passage in the *Elegy* with its neighbour bear careful
examination in this connection, for it is through his skilful
management of them that Pope establishes the reconciliations of
the poem on a *poetic* level. There are times when the poem is
made to hang (or seem to hang) on the 'if's and 'why else?'s' of
argument. Sometimes it appears to turn on a single word, as when
the word 'brave' permits Pope to make an imaginative leap from
paragraph 1 (with its suggestion that neither heaven nor earth has
a place for brave and passionate people) to the illogical argument
of paragraph 2 (that the Lady's fault being both divine and
heroic, she must necessarily have a place in the 'blest abodes').
We have already noticed the play, with similar effect, on the
word 'avails' in paragraph 6. Occasionally a transition is effected
by methods that look back to the models provided for the control
of emotion, by the classical tradition and by Milton.

Every poet of quality learns sooner or later that art of permanent value cannot be created without the equal involvement in its
making of mind and feeling, thought and sensibility, bringing
about the operation of that faculty we have come to think of as
the imagination. Pope learned his lesson sooner than most poets,
and he has left a record of his achievement in the *Elegy*. The
poem charts a process of continual temptation in the several
directions of emotional and intellectual self-indulgence, and a
development in spite of it towards balance and artistic discipline.
Achieving in its form an artistic approximation to the original
experience from which it sprang, the *Elegy* exists as much more
than a lament in traditional style for a dead personage of unusual
worth: by virtue of its finely modelled structure, it becomes an
exciting personal record of a poet's progress. It deserves regard,

not only for its patches of witty brilliance and emotional power, nor even for the poise and formal dignity of certain passages, but for the way it yields *when viewed as a whole* both evidence and record of a great poet's near-failure and ultimate success in fusing reason and feeling with a fiery energy that was to ensure his emotional and artistic growth.

When we stand back from the personal experience the *Elegy* embodies, and look again at the warring elements it succeeds in fusing or reconciling – pagan and Christian, an English eighteenth-century contemporaneity and a Roman Augustan past, sentimental melodrama and Metaphysical wit – we find that Pope has left us something more: an instance of the way a great poet concerned with exploring and resolving personal or artistic problems of his own, can sometimes reflect and resolve conflicts that exist outside his immediate interests, becoming an unconscious spokesman for his age.

6

'The life of a wit is a warfare upon earth'

To the development in imaginative and technical poetic power
revealed in the 'personal' poetry of *Windsor Forest, Eloisa to
Abelard* and the *Elegy* as they succeed each other, another work
supplied a continuous source of nourishment. This was Pope's
translation of Homer's *Iliad* and *Odyssey* into English verse,
undertaken with the help of public subscription and published in
parts during the eleven years between 1715 and 1726.

Joseph Addison, the critic and contemporary arbiter of English
letters, gave the young translator his encouragement only to with-
draw it later and bestow it on Pope's rival, Ambrose Philips, who
had also undertaken a translation of Homer. To the uneasiness
created by this incident, Pope's awareness of his own shortcomings
as a classical scholar added further difficulties; at times the task
of translation must have seemed a tedious burden. Leaving London for the country in 1715, Pope sardonically gave his reasons:

> Why should I stay? Both parties rage;
> My vixen mistress squalls;
> The wits in envious feuds engage;
> And Homer (damn him) calls.
> *A Farewell to London* (1715)

A heavy task, but worth doing, for Pope believed himself to be
working on the greatest poetry the world had ever seen. His mis-
sion was no less than the release of all that literary treasure into
English verse. He achieved it, creating in his translation what
amounted to a repertory or thesaurus of the poetic. Homer looms
large in the heritage of Dryden, Pope's predecessor, but the classical tradition might have come to an end in the early eighteenth
century had it not been prolonged by Pope into an active, lively
inheritance that was passed on to Crabbe and Byron.

The long-term rewards of the task included more mundane
matters too, for Pope's Homer brought him financial and literary
independence. In an age of flattering dedicators and rich patrons
ready to be tickled by their praise, Pope could steer a straight

course guided by his own firm conception of what was just and reasonable. Since this conception came to harmonise with the highest moral standards of his age, Pope's translation was very important indeed to his career as a poet. It was 'thanks to Homer' that he could

live and thrive   68
Indebted to no Prince or Peer alive.
Imitations of Horace, Book II,
Epistle II

– a matter for some gratitude when his mind began to turn more and more strongly from good-humoured Addisonian raillery to hard-hitting satire.

In translating Homer, Pope recreated *The Iliad* in terms of the sensibility of his own age. Placed in an Augustan world, Paris carries a spear with 'gallant grace', a panther's skin flows over the hero's armour with an 'easy pride', the squabbling Greek heroes are turned into sophisticated eighteenth-century English statesmen, and Axilus becomes an English country gentleman, the recognisable descendant of Chaucer's Franklin and the contemporary of Fielding's Squire Allworthy. As a translator, Pope has been called[1]

an impressionist: he gives us the felt impression of a whole scene or of the Homeric style rather than an accurate reproduction of the original text . . . (and is) quite free in making omissions and in supplying his own details . . . We must admire Pope's art in managing to be both polite and heroic . . . his gift for learning from Homer while maintaining his own style . . . Having English poetic conventions firmly in mind, and with his penchant for varying epithet and rhythm and for creating fine effects in imagery and imitative sound, Pope produces a series of musical and sensuous variations on the Heroic themes. He is 'realizing' Homer in terms of his own art and temperament.

Pope was, in his own words, endeavouring 'at something parallel, tho' not the same'.[2] Such alertness to the values and manners of his own age as Pope displays in his translation denied him the satisfactions of literal exactness in his rendering of Homer. Even had such exactness been attainable by a translator writing for another age in another language, the medium of the heroic couplet would have withheld it from Pope as it withheld from him

[1] By R. A. Brower, *Alexander Pope: The Poetry of Allusion* (1959, 1963) pp. 114–20.
[2] *The Iliad*, XIII, n. xxxix, v. 721.

the satisfaction of an exact representation of Eloisa's sufferings. The classical scholar Dr Bentley allowed that Pope had written a 'pretty poem', but denied him the right to call it Homer. Pope made Bentley pay for that comment with his portrait in *The Dunciad*, but there was truth in the remark. Pope's *Iliad* is Pope's poem, 'something parallel, tho' not the same' as Homer's great original. His long labours on it made more sure of itself the hand that was to undertake as its next work of importance the task of rendering into poetry the world of contemporary literature: in 1728 Pope published his own 'epic' poem in three books, *The Dunciad*, the work in which 'personal' and 'public' merge for the first time into one, and feeling of the most deeply felt kind is directed to serve standards set by Wit and Reason.

The purpose of *The Dunciad*, as it was first presented to the public, was punishment. In *A Letter to the Publisher occasioned by the present Edition of the Dunciad*, Pope's 'defender' William Cleland declared: 'Law can pronounce judgment only on open Facts, Morality alone can pass censure on Intentions of mischief; so that for secret calumny or the arrow flying in the dark, there is no publick punishment left, but what a good writer inflicts.' The 'Testimonies of Authors' that precede the poem introduce Pope's principal critics and partisans in a manner seemingly so impartial and unplanned that the reader comes away from them with an impression of many voices rising in clamorous confusion, upon which he supposes the poem itself will impose the necessary order. Scriblerus's preface to *The Dunciad* declares the poem to be of the epic kind, written by the translator of *The Iliad* as part of his duty to Homer, whose original comic epic had been 'lost'. (Readers of Fielding's novel, *Joseph Andrews*, will remember a similar anxiety on that author's part to establish a connection between his own 'comic epic' in prose and Homer's lost originator of the mode, *Margites*.) To substantiate his claims for *The Dunciad*, Scriblerus further informs the reader that the poem's action will be concerned with

the Removal of the Imperial seat of Dulness from the City to the polite world; as that of the Aeneid is the Removal of the empire of *Troy* to *Latium*. But as *Homer*, singing only the *Wrath* of *Achilles*, yet includes in his poem the whole history of the *Trojan* war, in like manner our author has drawn into this single action the whole history of Dulness and her children.

In further imitation of Homer, and in particular of his method of reversal in writing his comic epic, *The Dunciad* chooses its hero by virtue of his sheer insignificance and obscurity: he is to be the publisher Lewis Theobald, who has distinguished himself in each of the spheres specially patronised by 'Dulness', being at once a political journalist, a dull poet, and a 'wild critick'. In the last paragraph of the Scriblerus preface Pope puts forth a claim that is half serious, half self-mocking: he is writing this poem at the age of forty, 'the very *Acme* and pitch of life for Epic poesy'. He surrounds this claim with glancing humorous references to Blackmore, and even to Rymer and Dennis, indications (apparently) that we are not to take it too seriously. And yet a note regarding the poem's allusions to the ancients, which are said to be so 'alter'd and interwoven with the rest, that several have been, and more will be, by the ignorant abused, as altogether and originally his own', suggests that *The Dunciad* is more than an imitation, carrying within it such marks of family relationship that we would not be wrong in recognising even in the author's most original and seemingly characteristic passages, a blood-tie with the greatest of ancestors, Homer.

The presiding genius of *The Dunciad* is the goddess Dulness, given her 'correct' parentage as 'Daughter of Chaos and eternal Night' (I, 10). 'Dulness' for Pope had a specially sinister connotation. If we look back to *An Essay on Criticism*, we will remember that the critic who ignored the overall harmony and value of a work in order to pick upon its minor flaws was seen as possessed by a 'malignant dull Delight' (see page 1), and the very opposite of the just and 'gen'rous' judge. Theobald, who had censured Pope's edition of Shakespeare, must have seemed at the time the perfect anti-hero for a comic epic aimed at ridiculing the contemporary literary milieu. He is shown as the favourite of the goddess Dulness, who herself reigns in 'clouded Majesty' (I, 43), an early indication of the subtly, insultingly qualified epithets Pope will consistently use to describe her 'glories'. Her inherited characteristics stamp her own nature and define her natural sphere:

> Fate in their dotage this fair idiot gave,   I, 11
> Gross as her sire, and as her mother grave,
> Laborious, heavy, busy, bold, and blind,
> She rul'd, in native Anarchy, the mind.

We are soon to find them reflected in the characters of her chosen favourites. Her 'wild creation' (I, 80) is given spectacular and detailed treatment, so that the peculiar menace her power represents may be imaginatively established:

> Here she beholds the Chaos dark and deep,   I, 53
> Where nameless somethings in their causes sleep,
> 'Till genial Jacob, or a warm Third-day
> Call forth each mass, a poem or a play.
> How Hints, like spawn, scarce quick in embryo lie,
> How new-born Nonsense first is taught to cry,
> Maggots half-form'd, in rhyme exactly meet,
> And learn to crawl upon poetic feet.

The empire of Dulness is seen as a warm, teeming dung-heap, in which maggots and grubs in the form of perverse fancies are encouraged to develop, nonsense made audible, and all manner of graceless artistic excrescences woken out of their sleep. The literary faults Pope particularly abhorred are presented as an Olympian entertainment –

> There motley Images her fancy strike,   I, 63
> Figures ill-pair'd, and Similes unlike.
> She sees a Mob of Metaphors advance,
> Pleas'd with the Madness of the mazy dance:

Beyond the 'divine' court of Dulness, the population of this empire continues its misbegotten tradition, approved by the presiding deity who observes with pleasure

> How Tragedy and Comedy embrace;   I, 67
> How Farce and Epic get a jumbled race;

in a landscape that is itself entirely at odds with Nature and natural laws, where

> . . . Time himself stands still at her command,   I, 69
> Realms shift their place, and Ocean turns to land.
> Here gay Description AEgypt glads with showers;
> Or gives to Zembla fruits, to Barca flowers;
> Glitt'ring with ice here hoary hills are seen,
> There painted vallies of eternal green,
> On cold December fragrant chaplets blow,
> And heavy harvests nod beneath the snow.

Pope's wrath at the ignorant impudence that professes to make literature in defiance of the established laws of nature and reason vents itself in a tone of wondering amazement ('Time himself

stands still at her commmand!') and a sensuous verbal exposition
of that literature –

And héavy hárvests nód / beneath the snow –

that shows without need for further explanation how contradictory and nonsensical it is. The subtlety with which he uses the
classical original may be seen in his descriptive epithet (used of
Jupiter by Homer, and here applied to Dulness) of 'cloud-
compelling' majesty (I, 77). The magnificence of the phrase is
double-edged, for the words introduce the reader to the 'fogs' of
incomprehension, pedantry and vagueness that characterise the
literature of her Grub Street kingdom and remind him how
insignificant are the objects that are momentarily magnified and
dignified by mists and fogs.[3]

Many general features of *The Dunciad* will strike the reader of
The Rape of the Lock as familiar, especially the verbal, tonal and
situational parallels to the classical epic recognisable in the poem's
'heroic' soliloquies, the literary 'Olympiad' in Book II, and the
exchanges between gods and mortals throughout the work. The
voluminous notes, annotations and tongue-in-cheek cross-refer-
ences imitate and illustrate the academic pretensions and
pendantry of certain scholars who had made the mistake of attack-
ing Pope's edition of Shakespeare and his translation of *The Iliad*.
The comic portraits of individuals remind us of earlier work, the
portraits of 'Sir Plume' in *The Rape of the Lock* and the 'bookful
Blockhead' in *An Essay on Criticism*. But there is a difference.
Pope's use of the couplet is still compact and epigrammatic, but
his methods are closer to those of the novelist than of the witty
youthful writer of *The Rape of the Lock*. The literary 'world' of
The Dunciad's milieu is broader and more varied than the tiny,
self-contained, social *beau monde* of the earlier poem; the writers,
critics and publishers who people it are seen in more realistic and
lifelike terms. Not that the themes that concerned the poet of *The
Rape of the Lock* were less serious, for both works are deeply
involved with moral issues and with one in particular: the foolish
vanity that mistakes the trivial for the significant. But *The
Dunciad* is conceived on a far grander scale than any other of

---

[3] *An Essay on Criticism*, 392–3:
> As things seem large which we through Mists descry,
> Dulness is ever apt to magnify.

Pope's works. We become aware, while we read, of a varied and populous world, of events leisurely unfolding in a poem that will take its appropriate time to 'hatch a new Saturnian age of Lead' (I, 26).

The peculiar tensions of *The Dunciad* are apparent from its very beginning: we are embarking on a guided tour of a literary inferno, our Virgil a poet who scorns what he pretends to praise, who foresees and fears the possible future collapse of all he holds dear. The parallels with Swift's *Gulliver's Travels* are evident, except that in *The Dunciad* there is no 'innocent' mask, no 'gullible' *persona*. Instead we have a depersonalised voice that praises what reason would condemn, and denigrates what virtue would protect – the voice, indeed, of contemporary letters, the attitude of mind that Pope knew was replacing the discriminating, balanced reasonableness that had guided his age when it was at its best. The debased standards of a literary world that mistakes bombast for true poetry and finds prose virtues in bad verse, that trades reason for enthusiasm, 'simplifies' true learning with the aid of notes and an index, and – ignorant or uncaring of the cultural values of European tradition represented by Graeco-Roman civilisation and the contemporary achievements of France, except for purposes of plagiarism – finds its literary star in a Colley Cibber are caught by Pope in Book I, 227–40:

> Here to her Chosen all her works she shows;
> Prose swell'd to verse, Verse loit'ring into prose;
> How random Thoughts now meaning chance to find.
> Now leave all memory of sense behind:
> How Prologues into Prefaces decay,
> And these to Notes are fritter'd quite away.
> How Index-learning turns no student pale,
> Yet holds the Eel of Science by the Tail.
> How, with less reading than makes felons 'scape,
> Less human genius than God gives an ape,
> Small thanks to France and none to Rome or Greece,
> A past, vamp'd, future, old, reviv'd, new piece,
> 'Twixt Plautus, Fletcher, Congreve, and Corneille,
> Can make a Cibber, Johnson, or Ozell.

An impression of decay, lethargy and deformity (prefaces deteriorate, verse 'loiters', prose 'swells' as if it were diseased), is established by the quality of Pope's diction, its wealth of wide-ranging literary and contemporary allusion. He mercilessly makes his anti-hero pray that Dulness will continue her protection of himself and his works, that she will, being

> ever gracious to perplex'd mankind!   I, 151
> (Who) spread a healing mist before the mind,
> And, lest we err by Wit's wild, dancing light,
> Secure us kindly in our native night.

The classical parallel is scrupulously (and comically) pursued in Book II, where the Goddess celebrates the coronation of King Theobald with a series of public competitive sports, an Olympiad of Dulness. Pope's view of his Grub Street enemies as a race of dunces now extends to a presentation of selected individuals in laughable action: as in the portrait of the publisher Curl lumbering past his rival Lintot

> As when a dab-chick waddles thro' the copse,   II, 59
> On feet and wings, and flies, and wades, and hops;
> So lab'ring on, with shoulders, hands, and head,
> Wide as a windmill all his figure spread

that conveys visually and by means of the jog-trot movement of line 60, the impression a clumsy man of letters makes on a skilled and graceful writer. The 'waddling' and 'lab'ring' movements of Curl are reinforced throughout the poem by a multitude of equally vivid equations of contemporary literary activity with clumsy or irritating behaviour in the lower 'degrees' of the natural world. We have II, 247–50, in which the loud intoning of poetic 'Ass . . . to Ass' makes their 'brethren' in Tottenham fields twitch their hairy ears and forget to graze; or I, 169–72, in which Theobald declares his readiness for Dulness's sake to

> explain a thing till all men doubt it,
> And write about it, Goddess, and about it;
> So spins the silkworm small its slender store,
> And labours, 'till it clouds itself all o'er.

These are images that underline the aptness of the contemptuous term 'Grub Street' that Augustans applied to the journalistic hacks they despised, and look back to the opening picture in Book I of the special domain of Dulness, where

> Hints, like spawn, scarce quick in embryo lie   57

and

> Maggots half-form'd, in rhyme exactly meet,   59
> And learn to crawl upon poetic feet.

The other side of Pope's conception of the 'Games' in Book ii
is much less restrained, but equally effective in robbing his anti-
heroes of their dignity. The comedy of Book ii savours occasionally of the humorous practical joke, the wit of the music hall, and
the artistry of lavatorial graffiti; as in lines 65–100, where Curl in
full career slides in a pool of excrement, is pitied by Jove (seated
'easing' himself after an ambrosial feast) and is thereby refreshed:

> Renew'd by ordure's sympathetic force,
> As oil'd with magic juices for the course,
> Vig'rous he rises; from th'effluvia strong
> Imbibes new life, and scours and stinks along,
> Re-passes Lintot, vindicates the race,
> Nor heeds the brown dishonours of his face.

In ii, 159–82, two booksellers compete in a new field – that of
expert urination – the victorious effort being celebrated by Pope in
terms of the true heroic:

> Impetuous spread
> The stream, and smoaking, flourish'd o'er his head.
> So, (fam'd like thee for turbulence and horns,)
> Eridanus his humble fountain scorns,
> Thro' half the heav'ns he pours th'exalted urn;
> His rapid waters in their passage burn.

The loser is rewarded by the consolation prize of a china chamber-
pot. In ii, 183–212, the winner of a competition among authors
and dedicators as to who can best tickle a wealthy patron secures
Venus's help in his attempt, and is rewarded with the post of
Secretary to a Duke. The humour here is far from 'polite' in the
conventional sense, but its frankness is justified by the way it
permits the reader to share in the contempt Pope feels for what
he describes. To sustain the heroic parallel throughout a long
poem demands care and industry; employing animal or insect
parallels provides outlets for anger; but the opportunity Book ii
affords Pope to dip his opponents in bilge-water and rub their
noses in dung exercises other aspects of his attitude to his subject,
particularly his scorn for the denizens of Grub Street and his
personal sense of fun. It is never pointless fun, for each 'sinner'
is hoist with his own petard – Curl slips 'in the plash his wicked-
ness had lay'd' (72); the heroes who shamelessly urinate to public
applause are real-life rivals in impudence; and 'tickling' is an
appropriate euphemism for the kind of humiliating flattery that

the system of literary patronage encouraged and maintained. These unconventional incidents are described with a remarkable blend of physical realism and poetic traditionalism: we have only to turn back to Pope's *Essay on Criticism*, with its description of a nymph swiftly 'scouring' the plain (line 372) to recall that Pope is gracing Curl's performance with a term traditionally associated with speed. It is the wicked alliterative linking of 'scours' with 'stinks' that transmits Pope's real contempt for the 'hero' of the race: Curl has achieved a pre-eminence in a particular field that no man of sense would wish to take from him – for fear of what might rub off upon himself. Similarly the word 'smoaking', used unforgettably in *The Rape of the Lock* (III, 110) to liken the pouring of hot coffee to an epic flood, here lends a topsy-turvy dignity (together with suggestions of acute physical discomfort) to Curl's shameless display.

Nor is the humour of Book II, though frank, always or tiresomely explicit. A good deal is conveyed through ambiguous means, as in the innuendo by which the nature both of Jove's 'seat' and of the 'ichor' that distils from it is suggested (79–88). Equally ambiguous, though implicitly sexual, remains the precise method by which Venus's devotee wins the tickling competition. Such ambiguities are not the result of false delicacy on Pope's part but they do owe something to his use of the couplet's periphrastic possibilities in maintaining a smooth mock-heroic tone. By rendering Curl's triumphant vulgarity in epic terms, he prevents the descent of his own poem into the obscenity that it was designed to dissect and satirise. Since modesty has no place in the scheme of Grub Street's values, the impudence that rules in its stead must be exposed – but Pope achieves this purpose in strict conformity with (and within limits imposed by) the rules of mock-heroic writing. Pope's deliberate involvement of his antiheroes in physical and sexual indignities, very carefully maintaining the poem's overall poise in the very process of doing so by means of ambiguity, understatement and an unshakably elevated tone, is one way in which he overcomes the difficulties of his undertaking. For, as Scriblerus's preface makes abundantly clear, the difficulties are many and great: a poet 'might find it easier to paint a *Charlemagne*, a *Brute* or a *Godfry*, with just pomp and dignity heroic, than a *Margites*, a *Codrus*, a *Flecknoe*, or a *Tibbald*'. The references to Margites, Codrus, and Flecknoe are there to remind us of *The Dunciad*'s ancestry: the true descendant of Homer, Juvenal and Dryden is Pope, and in 'Tibbald' he is making his own contribution to the distinguished line of satire's anti-heroes.

The uninhibited intensity of contempt for contemporary scribblers that *The Dunciad* jets forth, its powerful invective, and in particular the detail of Book II, have all been criticised as the result of sadistic malice on the writer's part. No doubt Pope did pay off some old scores in writing the poem: Dennis, Gildon and Theobald reap in *The Dunciad* what they had sown in pamphlets, lampoons and criticism against him. Grub Street, which had not hesitated to make wanton fun of his deformities, squirms in *The Dunciad* with more than the insect-energy Pope ascribed to it. But in addition to its measure of personal malice, the poem expresses a profound concern for the current condition of English letters, a concern Pope shared with other members of the literary world. *The Dunciad* is a protest against the levelling down of literary standards, since this brings with it always a debasement of moral values. Pope saw and hated the intrusion of commerce into literature. He reacted strongly against the hack journalism of Grub Street for this reason, and personal venom adds power to his disgust. In a very real sense, therefore, as he himself wrote, the poem was not made for the contemptible authors it exposes, but the authors for the poem: strong personal antagonisms become in the end part of a larger aim. Though Pope derived the idea of *The Dunciad* from Dryden's *Mac Flecknoe* (see Chapter 4, pp. 50–2), making his own candidate Theobald succeed Dryden's enemy Thomas Shadwell upon the throne of Dulness, *The Dunciad* transcends both Dryden's poem and the limited area of personal attack and lampoon.

The duty of chastisement through satire was one Pope was often afterwards called upon to perform. In *A Letter to a Noble Lord, on occasion of some Libels written and propagated at Court in the Year 1732–1733* (1733) Pope addresses Lord Hervey in the tone of a patient adult addressing an impertinent schoolboy:

. . . Were it but the mere excess of your Lordship's wit, that carried you thus triumphantly over all the bounds of decency, I might consider your Lordship on your Pegasus, as a sprightly hunter on a mettled horse; and while you were trampling down all our works, patiently suffer the injury, in pure admiration of the noble sport. But should the case be quite otherwise, should your Lordship be only like a boy that is run away with; and run away with by a very foal; really common charity, as well as respect for a noble family, would oblige me to stop your career, and to help you down from this Pegasus.

Surely the little praise of a *writer* should be a thing below your ambition: you, who were no sooner born, but in the lap of the Graces; no sooner at school, but in the arms of the Muses; no sooner in the world, but you practised all the skill of it; no sooner in the court, but you possessed all the art of it! Unrivalled as you are, in making a figure, and in making a speech, methinks, my Lord, you may well give up the poor talent of turning a distich. And why this fondness for poetry? Prose admits of the two excellences you most admire, diction and fiction; it admits of the talents you chiefly possess, a most fertile invention, and most florid expression; it is with prose, nay the plainest prose, that you could best teach our nobility to vote, which you justly observe, is half at least of their business: and give me leave to prophesy, it is to your talent in prose, and not in verse, to your speaking, not your writing, to your art at court, not your art of poetry, that your Lordship must owe your future figure in the world.

The letter warns Hervey off the field of poetry, reminding him that the nobility have other things to do for society than bedevil it with bad verse. The balanced clauses work in this prose as the balanced couplets worked in Pope's *Dunciad*, to build an impression of utter contempt for the subject discussed. But the tone remains cool, never losing the easy casualness of conversation: 'And why this fondness for poetry? Prose admits of the two excellences you most admire, diction and fiction; it admits of the talents you chiefly possess, a most fertile invention, and most florid expression . . .' It is remarkably poised, for a writer of middle-class origins addressing a member of the English nobility. Only complete financial independence of the kind the success of *The Iliad* translation had secured for Pope could have guaranteed the personal safety of a writer who published such a letter in eighteenth-century England. And since such freedom was his alone to enjoy, it became at last a moral obligation (as well, of course, as a source of personal satisfaction) to use it in the service of English letters.

7

'That not in fancy's maze he wander'd long, but stoop'd to truth...'

An epistle, a poem written in the form of a letter, was an established literary form in the eighteenth century, with its own set of rules. The tone of such a poem was naturally influenced by the seriousness or levity of its theme, and by the nature of the poet's relationship with its dedicatee. In Pope's *Essay on Man* (see pp. 100–16), a dissertation composed in the form of four verse epistles addressed to Lord Bolingbroke, the seriousness of the subject decides the tone, which is solemn and dignified. Pope's reverence for Bolingbroke allows him to rise occasionally to heights of rhetorically expressed feeling, but never to drop to the easy, comradely exchanges that mark the *Epistle to Dr Arbuthnot* (see Chapter 8, pp. 121–34), where he discusses with an intimate friend the state of contemporary letters and his own career as a writer.

If an epistle was addressed to a high personage not intimately known to the author, this naturally influenced the poem's tone in the direction of formality, permitting elaborate compliment and some declamatory heightening to enter where appropriate: the epistles Pope addressed to Lord Burlington and Lord Bathurst on 'The Use of Riches' (see pp. 93–100) and to Viscount Cobham on 'The Characters of Men' (see pp. 117–18) illustrate this position. The gallant, complimentary style of Pope's *Epistle to a Lady* on 'The Characters of Women' (see Chapter 8, pp. 118–21) stands by itself: addressed to Pope's most affectionately regarded woman friend, and taking feminine foibles and contemporary manners and morals as its subject, the tone of the poem has a good deal in common with that of *To a Young Lady on her leaving the Town after the Coronation* (see Chapter 3, pp. 32–4).

Pope's style in these poems derives, like his models, from the Latin poet Horace, whose mixture of good sense, comic invention and pointed raillery had always delighted him with its 'graceful negligence',[1] and seems to have suited his own temperament better than the solemn, weighty style of Juvenal, the Roman satirist most imitated by Dryden. Reading the Moral Epistles and Essays Pope wrote between 1731 and 1735, we become aware through the very ease and poise of their conversational tone, of the existence of a group of clever, talented and purposeful men for whose eyes, primarily, he seems to have written. Dr Swift, John Gay, Dr Arbuthnot, Bolingbroke and others among Pope's circle of Tory friends believed in the power of literature to influence and enrich life, and their delight was in reading, writing, and talking about it. They live for us in Pope's Epistles and Essays as an Augustan literary intelligentsia, united by a strong sense of community and of shared standards, committed to struggle for the maintenance of sound values in public life and in the sphere of aesthetics. Describing the massive tastelessness of 'Timon's Villa', Pope alludes in his *Epistle to the Earl of Burlington* to

such a draught   103
As brings all Brobdignag before your thought.

The allusion to Book II of Swift's *Gulliver's Travels* would have registered instantly with the witty members of the 'Scriblerus Club' who provided the encouraging, appreciative audience both Swift and Pope enjoyed.

A book such as Swift's makes us aware that corruption crawled beneath the superficial dignity of British politics and economic 'policy' in the eighteenth century. Wealth was lavished on vulgar display, true sympathy by-passed in the interests of snobbery. Religion was becoming an empty pretence, literature falling into the hands of hacks, the arts being fostered by uncritical men of wealth and title who were dangerously susceptible (because of their pretensions to aesthetic taste) to flattery from unscrupulous third-raters. When Pope turned to 'moralize his Song', his morality based itself firmly on the Augustan virtues of Reason, Moderation, Decorum and Good Sense, viewing the corruption and the vulgar excesses of his age as negations of the moral codes of civilisation. The aim of the moral satirist being the burning away of falsity and corruption and the revelation of the dangers of false pride, Pope's Epistles and Essays attempt to identify the rotten pillars that weakened the Augustan façade, remove or

[1] Cf. *An Essay on Criticism*, 653–60.

repair them, restoring the building by these means to its original health and strength. Like Swift's,[2] Pope's satire points

> at no defect
> But what all mortals may correct

since, after all, the Augustan ideal was not an unattainable impossibility, but within the grasp of every man who practised the everyday virtues of sense and moderation.

In Pope's *Epistle to the Earl of Burlington* 'Of the Use of Riches' (1731), the Augustan moral codes are extended to become the standard by which art in everyday practical matters should be guided. The Earl was a man of influential, classically austere taste. A true admirer of Palladian architecture, he had rebuilt his own houses according to its rules; he had been responsible for publishing (and by this means, popularising) Palladio's architectural designs and drawings; and he had given his patronage to English architects and draughtsmen who shared his tastes and could translate his ideas into graceful reality. Pope's poem begins with a scornful survey of the artistic (and therefore moral) blunders made by Burlington's tasteless contemporaries in their efforts to rival him in the decoration of country houses and gardens. Crowned with the Latin names appropriate to a Horatian epistle, 'Virro' and 'Sir Visto' waste energy and money on buildings and gardens that, when completed, only expose their owners' lack of discrimination (lines 13–22).

Pope attacks the pretentiousness which imitates what it does not understand, and the bad taste of his 'improvers' reveals a moral flaw: anxious to

> Load some vain Church with old Theatric state,   29
> Turn Arcs of triumph to a Garden-gate;
> Reverse your Ornaments, and hang them all
> On some patch'd dog-hole ek'd with ends of wall,
> Then clap four slices of Pilaster on't,
> That, lac'd with bits of rustic, makes a Front.
> Or call the winds thro' long Arcades to roar,
> Proud to catch cold at a Venetian door;
> Conscious they act a true Palladian part,
> And if they starve, they starve by rules of art

they seize upon Burlington's beautiful and functional designs and turn them to ugly, inappropriate (and therefore immoral) use.

[2] Swift, *On the Death of Dr Swift* (1731).

Alexander Pope

Pope's description of 'Timon's Villa' sums up the principles of bad taste, indicating that beauty only keeps company with good sense. Detail after detail, presented in the rising rhythm and enthusiastic tone and phrase we associate with heroic praise, is shown to be the vulgar excrescence it is by precise placing of the most expressive word in the most telling position, and by skilful exploitation of the couplet's capabilities for emphasis and antithesis:

> Greatness, with Timon, dwells in such a draught   103
> As brings all Brobdignag before your thought.
> To compass this, his building is a Town,
> His pond an Ocean, his parterre a Down:
> Who but must laugh, the Master when he sees,
> A puny insect, shiv'ring at a breeze!

Timon's massive, exaggerated structures only reveal the poverty of his taste, hence the withering effectiveness of the next lines –

> Lo, what *huge heaps* / of *littleness* around!   109
> The whole, a labour'd Quarry above ground.

A conducted tour of the Villa grounds next examines the bad taste that takes classical regularity to the point of tedium –

> No pleasing Intricacies intervene,   115
> No artful wildness to perplex the scene;
> Grove nods at grove, each Alley has a brother,
> And half the platform just reflects the other.

The balanced rhythm of the couplet form adds emphasis here to the impression of weary monotony Pope wishes to convey, for the repeated sounds provide an aural parallel for visual regularity that seems to enact what is being described. A different method, that of using carefully chosen antitheses, is employed to balance a list of decorative elements with examples of their inappropriate use:

> The suff'ring Eye inverted Nature sees,   119
> Trees cut to Statues, Statues thick as trees,
> With here a Fountain, never to be play'd,
> And there a Summer-house, that knows no shade;
> Here Amphitrite sails thro' myrtle bow'rs;
> There Gladiators fight, or die, in flow'rs . . .

The tragi-comic absurdity of 'Trees cut to Statues' thus exists side by side with the other idiotic idea of planting the grounds with 'Statues thick [by which Pope probably meant 'numerous' rather than 'gross', but both meanings are obviously possible, and both equally appropriate] as trees'. The Villa gardens indeed provide a display of 'inverted Nature', and the eye of the sensitive visitor flinches before the distortion of what could have been beautiful if reasonably developed and properly cared for.

Once indoors, the poem takes up further outrages of taste which reveal disastrously bad judgment: the impressive 'study' filled with rare editions, the contents of which the owner knows and cares nothing about (lines 133–40); the chapel in which prayers are said in *pride*, and not in piety. Alliteration works here in Pope's characteristic way, linking together ideas that do not or (should not) have anything in common –

> And now the Chapel's silver bell you hear,   141
> That summons you to all the Pride of Pray'r:
> Light quirks of Musick, broken and uneven,
> Make the soul dance upon a Jig to Heaven.
> On painted Cielings you devoutly stare,
> Where sprawl the Saints of Verrio or Laguerre,
> On gilded clouds in fair expansion lie,
> And bring all Paradise before your eye.

The whole passage describes with the utmost sensuousness a pleasurably aesthetic, physical and emotional experience very far removed from the austerities of religious devotion: the saints on the painted ceiling 'sprawl' luxuriously 'in fair expansion' on 'gilded' clouds – a description more suited to the houris of an Islamic paradise than to the citizens of a sober Christian heaven. The staccato movement of 'light/quirks/of/Musick/bro-/ken/ and/uneven' provides the jigging accompaniment for these easy devotions, easier because immediately after the musical prelude,

> To rest, the Cushion and soft Dean invite,   149
> Who never mentions Hell to ears polite.

The 'softness' of the Dean's text and sermon indicate that he, too, is part of the chapel's expensive upholstery, a mere cushion interposed between the worshipper and the realities of real religion. His 'softness', like the luxuriousness of the 'Saints', suggests a rottenness at the core of all this outward splendour.

These precise effects are the result of the careful polishing –

what Keats called 'handicraftsman's' labour – which made it possible for Augustan poetry to be published in quantity without the glaring excesses of over-emotionalism and bad taste that scar a good deal of Romantic poetry in the years that followed. The moral virtue of Decorum becomes in Pope's poetry the literary virtue of *appropriateness*, the faculty of judging the right word or phrase for a given place, and the art of precisely fitting it in position. The same virtue governs the poem's final shape, for it guides the poet's relation of specific parts to his thesis as a whole, presiding over the poetic process from the moment Wit and Feeling have completed their inspirational role and begun to yield their place to poetic craftsmanship. We have seen Decorum at work in the final shaping of what might have been an untidy piece of emotionalism, Pope's *Elegy to the Memory of an Unfortunate Lady* (see Chapter 5). In this *Epistle* it provides the standard by which art is to be judged, presiding at the same time over the poet's fitting of technique to theme.

The poem goes on to consider other excesses, such as the dining-room decorations of Timon's Villa, which consist of extravagances so vulgar and revoltingly ugly that they put the diner off his food (lines 153–6). The details that make up the picture have been taken, not from a particular nobleman's residence, but from many such that Pope had visited. For characterising these details as examples of tasteless opulence and badly-used wealth, Pope was accused of insulting his hospitable acquaintances; of using his wit, his reputation and his towering talent irresponsibly to hurt those who had never harmed him; and of placing a burden of shame and ridicule on well-meaning, virtuous people. Swift had been similarly arraigned, his poem on his own death states his ironical conviction that his enemies will now

> revive the libels born to die;
> Which Pope must bear as well as I.

Both poets defended themselves from the charge that personal malice envenomed their satiric writing, both invoked the sanctity of the satiric mode and the moral purpose which alone justified it. The *Epistle to the Earl of Burlington* finds consolation in the thought that, all partial evil working in devious ways to universal good, even from Timon's pretentious and immoral wastefulness, some public benefit is immediately derived:

> Yet hence the Poor are cloath'd, the Hungry fed;   169
> Health to himself, and to his Infants bread
> The Lab'rer bears: What his hard Heart denies,
> His charitable Vanity supplies.

Regarded in the perspective allowed us by Time, the outrages perpetrated by Timon could even be seen as ephemeral. In some happier era, Nature will come into her own again and the distorted landscape be restored to beauty and usefulness:

> Another age shall see the golden Ear   173
> Imbrown the Slope, and nod on the Parterre,
> Deep Harvests bury all his pride has plann'd,
> And laughing Ceres re-assume the land.

Pope's *Epistle to Lord Bathurst*, also 'Of the Use of Riches' (1733), concerns itself with money and its proper use. It views wealth as a 'shining mischief' (line 10), bestowed by fortune indiscriminately on all sorts and conditions of men: the ownership of wealth can therefore be no sign in itself of unusual worth (lines 17–18), and it is in its use that virtue and good sense should make their influence felt. As in the earlier *Epistle* Pope suggests that Nature reconciles even such extremes as that adopted by 'old Cotta', who saves his money only in order that his son might waste it (lines 179–218):

> Ask we what makes one keep, and one bestow?   165
> That POW'R who bids the Ocean ebb and flow,
> Bids seed-time, harvest, equal course maintain,
> Thro' reconcil'd extremes of drought and rain,
> Builds Life on Death, on Change Duration founds,
> And gives th'eternal wheels to know their rounds.

More satisfactory examples of sense and morality that do not depend on Nature and time to uncover their benefactions are the noble Lord Bathurst, the poem's dedicatee, and the humbler Mr John Kyrle (known as 'The Man of Ross') whose several activities advance health and prosperity in their neighbours and increase their own moral worth. They know well

> That secret rare, between th'extremes to move   227
> Of mad Good-nature, and of mean Self-love

possessed by men of reason and feeling, who live according to a proper code of values, practising a way of life in which thrift and generosity stop short of miserliness and waste, uniting instead

> To balance Fortune by a just expence,   223
> Join with Oeconomy, Magnificence;
> With Splendour, Charity; with Plenty, Health.

To balance these portraits, Pope provides two more in effective
contrast.

The first of these is a *tour de force* of novelistic skill and observa-
tion, as the once-brilliant and successful Duke of Buckingham
breathes his last in sordid and miserable surroundings –

> In the worst inn's worst room, with mat half-hung,   299
> The floors of plaister, and the walls of dung,
> On once a flock-bed, but repair'd with straw,
> With tape-ty'd curtains, never meant to draw,
> The George and Garter dangling from that bed
> Where tawdry yellow strove with dirty red,
> Great Villiers lies . . .

The second is the comic parable of 'Citizen Balaam' that ends the
Epistle, having been interposed in such a way that (and at just
the point where) the reader is ready for the comic relief it offers.
It is a condensed biography, wedding setting to subject, for it is
precisely where

> London's column, pointing at the skies,   339
> Like a tall bully, lifts the head, and lyes

that the equally false and hypocritical hero of Pope's tale lives
and labours for his own advancement. Can virtue and wealth
co-exist? The examples of Lord Bathurst and of the Man of Ross
suggest that they can, and do. But each of these men shares his
wealth with others, which Citizen Balaam – although outwardly
charitable – does not do:

> Religious, punctual, frugal, and so forth;   343
> His word would pass for more than he was worth.
> One solid dish his week-day meal affords,
> An added pudding solemniz'd the Lord's:
> Constant at Church, and Change; his gains were sure,
> His givings rare, save farthings to the poor

Pope's wit makes use of the couplet's antithetical potential to
stress the contradictions inherent in Balaam's outward piety. The
offhand 'and so forth' makes nonsense of Balaam's claims to
virtue, and the next line rests in a delicate ambiguity: are we
being asked to admire this man's integrity and the immense trust
men place in him, or his dishonesty? – for he guarantees more

money than he can pay if called upon to do so. The linking of the
word 'solemniz'd' with the pudding that graces Balaam's Sunday
dinner ridicules his hypocritical air of religious austerity; and
this is quickly reinforced by the next couplet, with its mocking
alliterative stress on the dutiful regularity with which he pays his
respects to God and to Mammon –

> Constant at *Ch*urch, and *Ch*ange . . .

and the seemingly effortless rhythmic variation that shifts our
attention to another aspect of Balaam's character as half-rhymes
assist alliteration in linking his 'sure gains' with his 'rare givings'.
These are so arranged that even as the certainty of their occur-
rence is shown to arise directly from Balaam's regular activity in
business and religion, a caesural pause after 'rare' prepares us for
the final shaft at his avarice: the poor can content themselves with
farthings, an attitude that casts an extremely dubious light on
the 'plain-ness and 'good'-ness ascribed to Balaam in the portrait's opening lines.

The Devil gives Balaam the wealth by which he plans to
destroy him (lines 349–56). Now is the time for the sober citizen
to give thought to the wise management of his wealth; but the
moment passes unrecognised, and we watch him progress from
success to worldly success, from knighthood to directorship, his
rise eased by sharp practice and sound investment and comically
marked by an increase in certain favourite material comforts –

> And lo! two puddings smoak'd upon the board.   360

Sir Balaam gradually abandons even such piety as he had formerly
pretended, for a new spirit of aggressive self-confidence:

> Behold Sir Balaam, now a man of spirit,   375
> Ascribes his gettings to his parts and merit,
> What late he call'd a Blessing, now was Wit,
> And God's good Providence, a lucky Hit.
> Things change their titles, as our manners turn:
> His Compting-house employ'd the Sunday-morn;
> Seldom at Church ('twas such a busy life)
> But duly sent his family and wife.

The 'spirit' that possesses him is now no longer even partially
that of God, but wholly of the Devil. And so begins the fall, as
Sir Balaam's second wife persuades him to forsake his sober
business habits for an extravagant life of fashion. From this

self-abandonment to Vanity follows the rapid destruction of his family, and his own public disgrace and death (lines 389–402). Left to himself, Balaam might have lived and died a grave and respectable, if hypocritical, businessman. But the Devil's mischievous gift of wealth has been his undoing. Lacking moral 'sense' and human feeling, Balaam's social advancement destroys him completely and a sizeable section of society with him. The liveliness and sheer comic delight with which the tale is told take nothing away from its seriousness. The *Epistle* voices concern that those to whom wealth brings power and influence should strive to use these advantages wisely, for the general good.

This, and other moral concerns that preoccupied Pope in his mature years, are codified in *An Essay on Man* (1733–4), and become increasingly the starting-point for his poetry and its exercise. To the question: Why did Pope express this code in verse? the poet has provided the answer in an address to his reader that precedes the poem. His reasons were two: the first – 'principles, maxims, or precepts so written, both strike the reader more strongly at first, and are more easily retained by him afterwards'; and the second – 'I found I could express them more *shortly* this way than in prose itself; and nothing is more certain, than that much of the *force* as well as *grace* of arguments or instructions, depends on their conciseness.'

He expands this to say he wished to strike a balance between detail and ornament, between ratiocinative argument and imaginative, poetic impressions. Pope is offering not a system of ethics only, but a poem that unites the two great literary positives of the Augustans, Wit and Reason. He concerns himself in it with the moral positive of Nature, which regards man as an inseparable part of the Universe; with Truth, which sees God as being at the centre of that Universe, causing it to function in accordance with the Divine will and purpose; and with Decorum, the behaviour and conduct appropriate to man as part of such a Universe.

An Essay on Man is a dissertation: that is, it is a generic piece of writing, a poem deliberately structured according to the rules governing the 'essay' or traditional classical oration. If we examine Epistle 1 of the *Essay* from this point of view, we will find there that Pope keeps closely to tradition's requirements, providing the *exordium* that prepares the mind of the audience to favour orator and oration (I, 1–16); *narratio*, that states the problem in brief (I, 17–42); *probatio*, containing the bulk of the argument, setting up the terms that will be used, advancing the proofs (I, 43–112); *refutatio*, that brings together objections to the argument and answers to these objections (I, 113–280); and *peroratio*, that sums up the argument (I, 281–94). This is all conscientiously and deliberately done. But Pope introduces a variation that ultimately changes the character of his poem and makes it very much his own creation, by writing his 'essay' in the form of a letter addressed to his friend, the statesman Bolingbroke. This was done presumably because the ideas expressed in the poem had emerged and developed in the course of discussions between Pope and Bolingbroke, and because the use of the epistolary or letter-form would allow him the argumentative tone necessary to his subject without damaging the structure of the essay-form. The general effect of this innovation is to replace formality with informality, oratory with a cultivated, conversational tone:

> Bring then these blessings to a strict account,   IV, 269
> Make fair deductions, see to what they mount.
> How much of other each is sure to cost;
> How each for other oft is wholly lost;
> How inconsistent greater goods with these;
> How sometimes life is risq'd, and always ease:
> Think, and if still the things thy envy call,
> Say, would'st thou be the Man to whom they fall?

The main body of the *Essay on Man* consists of a similar questioning and turning over of ideas, so that we seem to be accompanying the poet on a contemplative journey, reasoning our way into a code of ethics that can serve us as a guide to living. The structure of the *Essay* presents a picture of man in relation to his universe in Epistle I that is referred to in the course of Epistles II, III and IV, so that each succeeding part of the poem builds upon what has gone before and is interconnected with every other part, all the threads being tied together at the end of Epistle IV. The poem moves, therefore, by means of transitions that are sometimes logical, sometimes both logical and imaginative. We might be put in mind by it of Pope's structuring of the *Elegy to the Memory of an Unfortunate Lady*, with the difference that in the earlier poem he sought through skilful transitions to mirror the movements of private emotion (see Chapter 5) and in the *Essay* he imitates with their help the shifts of argument and conversation. When, in Epistle III or IV, we are 'reminded' of something that was debated and resolved in Epistle I or II, it has the effect on us and on our apprehension of the poem that memory has when we cast back in the midst of a conversation for the support of a point established a little earlier.

Pope wrote of this poem:

If I could flatter myself that this Essay has any merit, it is in steering betwixt the extremes of doctrines seemingly opposite, in passing over terms utterly unintelligible, and in forming a *temperate* yet not *inconsistent*, and a *short* yet not *imperfect* system of Ethics.

His intention to compromise is clear in his tentative manner and the hesitant negatives he employs – 'temperate *yet not* inconsistent', 'short *yet not* imperfect'. In spite of this hesitancy, and the generally thoughtful and reasonable tone adopted in the *Essay* itself, he does at times take there very high ground indeed in addressing his reader:

> All Nature is but Art, unknown to thee;   I, 289
> All Chance, Direction, which thou canst not see;
> All Discord, Harmony, not understood;
> All partial Evil, universal Good:
> And, spite of Pride, in erring Reason's spite,
> One truth is clear, 'Whatever IS, is RIGHT.'

If this kind of tone were consistent throughout the poem, the *Essay* would indeed be as 'intolerable' as some critics have found it.[3] But Pope uses this impressive manner and tone generally for the peroration with which he ends an epistle. Judiciously placed, such passages indicate through the conviction their tone conveys the poet's satisfaction with the conclusions reached in the *Essay*. However doubtful or tentative might have been the steps by which each conclusion was reached, he is certain at the end that it is the right one – for him, and for his age – and he offers it to us as a workable, reasonable, moderate system, an ethical code acceptable to Everyman.

The *Essay* should be judged, however, not only as a dissertation

---

[3] See, for example, F. R. Leavis, *op. cit.*: 'No one, I imagine, willingly reads through the *Essay on Man*. Pope piquing himself on philosophical or theological profundity and acumen is intolerable . . .'

but as a poem. Pope's cautious apology for using poetic methods cites brevity as one of his reasons: the brevity made possible by poetic images that condense and compress what it might have taken a philosopher pages of prose to define. At its very start the *Essay* leaps at once into an image that strikes the perfect note for Pope's theme of unity in diversity, one that proves itself capable of expansion and exploration as the argument develops, illuminating the argument and being illuminated by it: the image of a garden –

> A mighty maze! but not without a plan;   I, 6
> A Wild, where weeds and flow'rs promiscuous shoot,
> Or Garden, tempting with forbidden fruit.

As any eighteenth-century gentleman interested in gardening (and Pope was one) knew, a maze is an interesting and exciting place. One can get lost in it and become quite desperate unless one keeps one's head, for on all sides the green closes in on one till escape seems impossible. And yet this experience is the result of careful planning on the part of a landscape gardener, who has placed this tree just so, and another bush in that particular spot. So the diversity of natural creation, the many strange things of which the world seems to be made up – some beautiful, some frightening, all fascinating – may be the result of careful planning; and this the poem will justify, 'vindicating' the ways of the unseen planner to Man, who stumbles on without a guide. The image of the 'maze' widens almost at once from a particular, ingeniously constructed part of an English garden, to become the garden as a whole. And it is a garden such as the eighteenth century delighted in, when so many landowners planned their grounds as a source of aesthetic and intellectual pleasure, providing a series of effects (masked by groves and curving walks) that successively pleased the visitor's eye or surprised him into thoughtfulness or pleasant melancholy. From a 'Wild, where weeds and flow'rs promiscuous shoot' we turn to a 'Garden, tempting with forbidden fruit': from apparently uncontrolled natural landscape to a cultivated orchard.

The original image is taking on a variety of associations – the word 'promiscuous' means 'disorderly' in Pope's usage, but there creeps in already the associated idea of sexual and moral disorder. In a different way the words 'tempting' and 'forbidden' remind us of events in the Garden of Eden as described in Genesis 3, i–vi, and in Milton's *Paradise Lost*. They carry moral overtones, even while the surface meaning of the lines merely contrasts natural profusion with cultivated orderliness. They suggest that the world around us is not only diverse in natural phenomena, but in human condition.

The next lines suggest a spirit of comradely adventure:

> Together let us beat this ample field, 7
> Try what the open, what the covert yield;

'Beating' the field or countryside is an idiom derived from hunting, in which sport bushes and coverts are 'beaten' or disturbed, in the hope that wild fowl – a pheasant or a gamecock – will rise from it and give the hunter a sporting chance of shooting it. Here, then, is another part of God's garden, an area capable of yielding living objects of interest; and carrying on the hunting image, Pope promises to fix what he sees permanently in poetry. We will, he promises, see Man in the social aspects that yield examples of both Folly and Morality, a promise that looks back to lines 11 and 12 –

> The latent tracts, the giddy heights explore
> Of all who blindly creep, or sightless soar

– which could have been (and certainly includes) an allusion to the lower animals and reptiles, some of whom creep blindly, in the dark, guided by their senses of smell, touch or hearing; and to the birds, who fly high above the sight of man. But a closer examination suggests that Man's folly and his moral behaviour are included in the animal/bird allusion: it is Man, the ignorant, dull-witted fool, 'creeping blindly' along, lost to the beauties of the world, that the poem will 'catch'; it is Man, so proud, so ambitious that he is tempted to fly above the bounds set for human intellect, not only lost to common sight but himself blinded and 'sightless' to his true place in Nature, that the poem will 'shoot'. And we note that Pope and Bolingbroke, the walkers in this garden, are men behaving with true 'decorum' in the state appropriate to Man, using their bodies in healthful exercise, using their senses to enjoy the natural world around them, using their intelligence to reason out the meaning of what they see. Their reactions are decorous too, in the proper eighteenth-century sense of being appropriate – they will 'laugh' where they must, be 'candid' or honest and sympathetic where the sight demands it. And in all things they will see the hand of their Creator reflected.

We might notice in passing that the licence for Pope's treatment of pedants and bad writers in *The Dunciad* and in the *Satires* as clumsy animals, insects, reptiles and river-birds is provided in this passage in his *Essay on Man*. Here a parallel is drawn between men and the lower animals. It helps us to appreciate the moral conviction behind Pope's satire, and understand why what might seem mere skilled name-calling to us (who have lost the particular view of our universe as a great Chain of Being from which Pope worked) carried the weight of moral denunciation for an eighteenth-century reader.

Epistle I praises Reason as the particular attribute that separates Man from other animals, and the faculty by which (used properly) he can understand his true position in Nature. In working out this argument, Pope slips into many factual errors, e.g. he accepts the notion popular in his time, that lions have a defective sense of smell and hunt by ear (line 213); that the lynx's acute vision depends on rays sent out from its eye (212); he reflects the old belief that honey is a dew that falls on flowers (220); that the world is less perfect since the fall of Adam and Eve in Eden (147); he makes use of the common symbolical belief that Man's sight, unlike that of animals, is formed to look upwards (196); that odours communicate with the brain through streams of invisible particles or 'effluvia' (199); that the fly's eye has microscopic powers (194); that men, unlike angels, cannot hear the music of the spheres (202) . . . this list can be almost endlessly expanded. But true or false, these ideas (which, expressed in scientific prose might have doomed Pope's *Essay* to oblivion as being factually in error) carry the argument irresistibly along as poetry, because they make their appeal to our reason through our senses, and through Pope's extraordinary ability to communicate poetically a sensuous apprehension of what he has assimilated intellectually and imaginatively. The point about 'effluvia', for example, is unforgettably caught in sensuous terms, as the poet asks Man to consider what he would gain from possessing senses so fine that the merest touch would cause him acute agony –

> Or touch, if tremblingly alive all o'er, 197
> To smart and agonize at ev'ry pore?
> Or quick effluvia darting thro' the brain,
> Die of a rose in aromatic pain?

Similarly, in communicating his vision of the Great Chain of
Being, Pope's imagination fires to throw off poetry that creates its
own truth, a truth so convincing in itself that it can transcend
the philosophy it embodies, or substitute for it. We might violently
disagree, from the standpoint of our new awareness of Man's
gradual destruction of his environment and especially of its
animal-life, with lines like

> Far as Creation's ample range extends,   207
> The scale of sensual, mental pow'rs ascends:
> Mark how it mounts, to Man's imperial race,
> From the green myriads in the peopled grass:

Destructive as we know him to be, indifferent and hostile to the
creatures around him, Man has no claim to the title of 'emperor',
which has always carried with it ideas of mutual obligation and
responsibility, of protection and concern as well as of domination.
But we can hardly deny the poetic truth contained in the
dramatic rhythmic sweep that takes in – in four lines – the
teeming space between Man and Insect; or the peculiar, sensuous awareness of moving, unseen, microscopic yet multitudinous
life contained in the phrases 'green myriads' and 'the peopled
grass'. As the passage goes on, the accepted philosophical truisms
upon which Augustan civilisation rested become a vision that
a poet has seen with religious, and transmits with poetic, fervour –

> See, thro' this air, this ocean, and this earth,   233
> All matter quick, and bursting into birth.
> Above, how high progressive life may go!
> Around, how wide! how deep extend below!
> Vast chain of being, which from God began,
> Natures aethereal, human, angel, man,
> Beast, bird, fish, insect! what no eye can see,
> No glass can reach! from Infinite to thee,
> From thee to Nothing!

How firmly Pope held the belief that a single link struck from this
'chain' damages the whole structure of Creation can be judged
if we turn to *The Dunciad*, in which the whole picture of cultured,
light-giving activity overrun by the powers of Dulness takes its
vigour from Pope's moral view of an ordered universe (see
Chapter 1, pp. 5–6; Chapter 9, pp. 145–6). From this conviction
springs the view that

> All are but parts of one stupendous whole,   267
> Whose body, Nature is, and God the soul;

on which in turn is built the moral lesson taught by Epistle 1:

> Know thy own point: This kind, this due degree   283
> Of blindness, weakness, Heav'n bestows on thee.
> Submit – In this, or any other sphere,
> Secure to be as blest as thou canst bear:
> Safe in the hand of one disposing Pow'r,
> Or in the natal, or the mortal hour.

Our hindsight may tell us: this is merely social and political propaganda deriving from medieval origins, and designed to keep thrones safe for Tudor, and later for Stuart and Hanoverian monarchies. The rigid system of social distinctions that existed in the eighteenth-century England for which this poem was written might strike us, inheritors of what we like to think of pleasantly as social democracies, as immoral and hostile to individual liberty of thought and action. Their own system did not strike the Augustans as immoral or over-rigid, however; on the contrary, they believed it to be the ultimate in reasonableness and proper morality. Once we have recognised this way of thinking as natural to its time, limited as that time was by certain habits of religious thought, political institutions, social customs, and a restricted knowledge of the world outside Europe, we can see how the social divisions that kept every man in his place were seen at the time as sacred, at once reflecting and justified by the visible patterns of the stars in the skies. We can see how these social divisions could be supported by the naturalist's experience of animal-life and plant-life being divisible into kinds and families; and even by the unseen but imaginable orders of Angels, Cherubim and Saints in the Christian heaven. Man's task in this world was seen as being the imitation of God, and the development of a way of life that inclined neither to the bestial and animalistic in his nature nor overmuch to divine pretension. As Pope put it himself, in a discourse on good living,

> He knows to live who keeps the middle state,
> And neither leans to this side, nor to that.

Augustans would have agreed (and in fact did agree) with this statement, not so much because they were all perfect models of decorum and moderation, but probably because they sensed in their own nature – only too human – the constant temptation to veer away from the ideal of balanced perfection. The Augustan ideals of Reason, Moderation, Decorum, the ideal of the Golden Mean or Middle Way were ideals deliberately sought after by those who saw Man's position as special because he owned the gift of Reason, the attribute that kept him steadily poised above the bestial.

Epistle II of the *Essay on Man* is concerned with Man's abilities, weaknesses, emotions, and his nature which Pope conceived of as belonging to 'the middle kind', an idea we understand better in the light of what we have gathered from Epistle I. An interest in plumbing the depths of his own personality is appropriate to Man, who should not presume to use the gift of Reason in order to 'scan' or measure the ways of God. Again an image establishes the point of departure:

> Plac'd on this isthmus of a middle state,   II, 3
> A being darkly wise, and rudely great:

and we see once again how poetry compresses and reinforces the idea of balance, of being poised midway between one extreme and the other, using this time the resources of sound, rhythm and rhyme. The heroic couplet is, as we have seen, very appropriate to argument by virtue of its rhyming lines, since the rhymes lend emphasis to particular points, helping the poet to lead up by stages to some telling conclusion and then drive it home. And again, the fact that the lines are arranged in pairs helps argument since one line can carry an idea to which the pair-line proposes an opposing or supporting concept –

> Could he, whose rules the rapid Comet bind,   35
> Describe or fix one movement of his Mind?

Each line could be further subdivided by a pause or caesura that can split it neatly in two, or be placed a little nearer the start or end of a line as the poet wishes, in order to give subtler effects of balance, and embody different aspects of the developing argument:

> With too much knowledge for the Sceptic side,   5
> With too much weakness for the Stoic's pride,
> He hangs between; in doubt to act, or rest,
> In doubt to deem himself a God, or Beast;
> In doubt his Mind or Body to prefer,

> Born but to die, and reas'ning but to err;
> Alike in ignorance, his reason such,
> Whether he thinks too little, or too much:
> Chaos of Thought and Passion, all confus'd;
> Still by himself abus'd, or disabus'd;
> Created half to rise, and half to fall;
> Great lord of all things, yet a prey to all;
> Sole judge of Truth, in endless Error hurl'd:
> The glory, jest, and riddle of the world!

By an extremely sensitive fitting of the resources of his metre to the twists and turns of argument, Pope leads us from an apparently simple praise of Man to a true appraisal of the complex, muddled, yet oddly heroic creature that he is. Skilfully placed median pauses reinforce and rhythmically illustrate the points of the argument: we might look, for example, at the effect created after two unbroken, perfectly symmetrical lines that echo one another –

> With too much knowledge for the Sceptic side,
> With too much weakness for the Stoic's pride,

by the placing of the median pause in the line that follows:

> He hangs between;

so that rhythm visually and aurally enacts the nature of Man's dilemma. This is followed by a series of opposed concepts that share lines or half-lines, in which they parallel, balance, or alternate with one another –

> in doubt to act, / or rest, /
> In doubt to deem himself a God, / or Beast; /
> In doubt his Mind / or Body to prefer, /
> Born but to die, / and reas'ning but to err; /

in the disposal of which Pope's skill is directed towards avoiding tedium, inevitable if each were to be expressed in exactly the same manner. But he goes further, reinforcing each idea with a *rhythmic* truth that we accept even before we understand it. The rising rhythm that leads us from idea to idea and line to line carries through the concept of the 'middle state', so that it illuminates the thesis as a whole, the point of which is Man's intermediary moral position –

> Sole Judge of Truth, in endless Error hurl'd:
> The glory, jest, and riddle of the world!

Man's proper pursuit, arising from this position, is to reason his way between the extremes in his own and in general Nature, towards greater and greater self-knowledge.

In Epistle II Pope draws his illustrations from the scientific experiments of his own and earlier times; he alludes to the calculations being made to measure the earth and 'weigh' air by Robert Boyle, Torricelli and others; to the efforts made by Sir Isaac Newton and continued by other scientists, to determine the causes and operation of tidal movements in the ocean (20); to the attempts made by Newton, Halley and others to chart planetary movements (21); to the practice of astronomers who 'corrected' the inequalities of ordinary or natural time in order to work out the rules of planetary motion (22). This kind of scientific acumen Pope sees as remarkable but not necessarily virtuous or praiseworthy, since it carries with it a permanent temptation to intellectual pride. So he cuts it down to size with a picture of the angels in heaven marvelling at Newton's cleverness in explaining the mechanism of God's universe, as men point and wonder at a freak or a trained circus animal –

> Superior beings, when of late they saw   31
> A mortal Man unfold all Nature's law,
> Admir'd such wisdom in an earthly shape,
> And shew'd a NEWTON as we shew an Ape.

The reality, the generality of Man, suggests Pope, is altogether of another kind. Aspiring to god-like knowledge and dignity, given Reason that tempts him to higher and higher flight, Man is continually pulled down by forces within himself that co-exist with Reason: Passion, and the passionate impulses of uncontrolled feeling. The rest of Epistle II develops this thesis, of Man as involved in a moral conflict between Reason and Passion. Fixed by Reason at a particular point as the heavenly bodies are kept in space by the force of gravitation, Man is at the same time propelled by Self-Love and Passion and as a result keeps moving, just as contrary forces operate to keep the planets in orbit. This concept is expressed by poetic means, a broken, clogged rhythm illustrating the restraining effects of Reason –

> Fix'd / like a plant / on his peculiar spot, /   63
> To draw nutrition, / propagate, / and rot; /

while an arresting, dramatic image of fire and irresistible force

supported by a flowing, rapid rhythm, embodies the uncontrolled
hurtle of Passion –

> Or, meteor-like, flame lawless through the void, 65
> Destroying others, by himself destroy'd.

From this imaginatively apprehended picture of Reason and
Passion locked in eternal opposition, emerges Pope's answer to
the contemporary debate as to which of the two were best
equipped to govern the human personality. Pope sees Man's best
and most proper course as lying in the direction of controlled
Passion and strengthened, fortified Reason (77–80), giving the
virtues of each full value, but advising emphasis on the controlling powers of Reason and good Sense. External events endanger
the human personality, but they test it too and so are to be
welcomed and not avoided, for Man resembles Nature in containing storm and peace within his own personality. Man reflects
Nature as Nature includes Man, and gales are as necessary to both
as maps and compasses. Man's duty is to achieve an inner harmony of all his powers, a blending of Reason with Passion that
reflects the composite picture we call 'weather' in external nature,
in which tempest and fair weather alternate and co-exist:

> Love, Hope, and Joy, fair pleasure's smiling train, 117
> Hate, Fear, and Grief, the family of pain;
> These mix'd with art, and to due bounds confin'd,
> Make and maintain the balance of the mind:
> The lights and shades, whose well accorded strife
> Gives all the strength and colour of our life.

From here Pope moves to the idea of a ruling passion planted
in the human personality that grows with Man from infancy to
age, and can turn him in a single, dangerously limited, direction
(133–44). We will see Pope's theory of the ruling passion more
fully explored in a later work, the *Epistle to Viscount Cobham*
(see Chapter 8, pp. 117–18), and have already seen it used at
the close of the *Elegy to the Memory of an Unfortunate Lady*
(see Chapter 5, pp. 76–7) to reconcile conflicting emotions born of
Reason and Passion. The latter poem has prepared us, in its way,
for Pope's formal answer in his *Essay* to the dangers of the 'ruling
passion'; treat it as a friend, and gradually make of it a virtue.
This point, which would have taken much time and labour to
explain, is deftly presented by the skilful use of another poetic

device, the epigram: in this case, the epigrammatic tendencies of the heroic couplet. The whole point of an epigram is that it expresses something wittily, surprisingly and paradoxically, that on reflection turns out to be – if not exactly obvious – something we perfectly agree with in any case. Pope develops an image appropriate to his theme, the effects of grafting on a barren fruit-tree; with the help of epigrammatic style and method, the image reinforces the philosophical theory he has outlined:

> As fruits ungrateful to the planter's care   181
> On savage stocks inserted learn to bear;
> The surest Virtues thus from Passions shoot,
> Wild Nature's vigor working at the root.
> What crops of wit and honesty appear
> From spleen, from obstinacy, hate, or fear!
> See anger, zeal and fortitude supply;
> Ev'n av'rice, prudence; sloth, philosophy;
> Lust, thro' some certain strainers well refin'd,
> Is gentle love, and charms all womankind:
> Envy, to which th'ignoble mind's a slave,
> Is emulation in the learn'd or brave. . .
> The same ambition can destroy or save,
> And make a patriot as it makes a knave.

The Epistle ends as it began, expatiating on Man's essential foolishness: Man, who can be so mistaken as to doubt the existence of extreme vice and true virtue (therefore Idealism and Cynicism are equally dubious positions), think himself free from vice, or believe a neighbour deeper in the mire than he is. Fortunately, Pope suggests, Man's individual errors are corrected and brought into line by the invisible working out of God's master-plan for the whole of mankind, and this 'counter-works each folly and caprice', disappoints 'th'effects of ev'ry vice', and builds Man's prosperity on his weaknesses (lines 231–48). As an illustration Pope shows how Man, conscious of his own inadequacy, calls on the help of others, cementing in this way a strong and lasting social community (249–56). And as Man grows older and less able to contribute to the society his own needs and abilities have initiated and supported, he learns to accept his own weakness and resign himself to death (257–60).

The foolishness of man is capable of ironic application as well. His contentment with what he has and his reluctance to change places with another are ironically glanced at in lines 261–70 (see

Chapter I, p. 16, where this passage is examined in detail). A final survey of Man as dupe clinches the argument against temptation to intellectual arrogance. It reminds us of the speech Shakespeare puts into the mouth of the affected cynic, Jaques, in *As You Like It*. Pope's study carries a sharper bite, a less kindly view of Man's frailties:

> Behold the child, by Nature's kindly law,   275
> Pleas'd with a rattle, tickled with a straw:
> Some livelier play-thing gives his youth delight,
> A little louder, but as empty quite:
> Scarfs, garters, gold, amuse his riper stage;
> And beads and pray'r-books are the toys of age:
> Pleas'd with this bauble still, as that before;
> 'Till tir'd he sleeps, and Life's poor play is o'er!

This is Man seen from above, as if by the pitying eye of God or Nature, to which the most dignified prelate with his doctoral scarf, or nobleman with his Star and Garter, appear as little children. Man is always tempted to, and capable of, self-deception and vanity –

> These build as fast as knowledge can destroy;   287
> In Folly's cup still laughs the bubble, joy;

How fortunate, then, that God's wisdom overrides human error, working with him when he is capable of controlling his passions with Reason, and when he can no longer do this, working his inadequacies into a larger pattern!

Epistle III invites its readers, 'Look round our World', and the sight presented to them is the chain (already met with in Epistle I) that binds all things to one another in an interdependent society. Man, suggests the Epistle, would be foolish if he were to suppose that the earth existed for his good alone, since happiness is visibly enjoyed by all created things, and it is only incidentally that Man benefits by their happiness: by the joy birds have in singing, by the delight horses take in speed. Man's labours produce wheat in his fields – but that wheat benefits the birds (who do not contribute to its production) as much as the oxen (who do). In this interdependent world, Pope sees Man as carrying the greatest responsibility since he is the 'wit' – i.e. the intelligence – among animals, and capable of appreciating their beauty in a way animals of other species cannot. For various reasons, some of them selfish – pride, hunger, pleasure, curiosity –

Man protects and preserves the life that surrounds him. He is further blessed by being able to understand and even expect the approach of his own death, without having his actions paralysed by the thought of it. Animals for their part, since they are deprived of Reason, have the blessing of Instinct, and this is traditionally seen as evidence of God working for good in the animal world. It is this instinct, of a divine origin, that directs the building of a spider's web, and the nesting techniques of a kingfisher.

Now Nature becomes, by an easy transition, more limited in scope to the character of individual or species. We are told that all creatures, whatever their element, propagate their kind, nurse it, and launch it on its way. Man's ties are seen to last longer than those of most animals, since they are strengthened by the faculty of Reason and by the prompting of custom and form. A picture of the Golden Age follows, of man living harmoniously with beasts, his temples peaceful, his diet vegetarian, his manner of life devoid both of pomp and of the artistic activity that promotes pomp. The implication is that this simplicity was God-given; it was what God wanted for Man, who in later times perverted the divine intention –

> Ah! how unlike the man of times to come!   III, 161
> Of half that live the butcher and the tomb;
> Who, foe to Nature, hears the gen'ral groan,
> Murders their species, and betrays his own.

and brought about his own lasting punishment:

> But just disease to luxury succeeds,   165
> And ev'ry death its own avenger breeds;
> The Fury-passions from that blood began,
> And turn'd on Man a fiercer savage, Man.

The next stage sees Man's reason operating slowly to imitate instinctual inclinations in animals – he learns to sail like the nautilus, to build like the bee, to form a social community like that of the ant. And even though Man may over-refine what he learns, he attains in this way to a superior place among the animals, absorbing their talents and skills, and evolving further the institutions of state, of monarchy, and of patriarchal government. Self-love operates, therefore, to the public good. The Epistle ends on the Aristotelian note that forms of government should be judged according to their effectiveness in promoting the happiness of the individuals they control. Integrity is a prerequisite –

> Thus God and Nature link'd the gen'ral frame, 317
> And bade Self-love and Social be the same.

In Epistle IV, having considered Man in relation to (I) the Universe, (II) his individuality and (III) society, *An Essay on Man* turns to a study of Man with respect to happiness. Of divine origin, a 'celestial seed', where does it grow among mortals? The learned blindly dispute where happiness can be found. Its benefits are obvious, 'in no extreme they dwell', and right-thinking and good intentions can bring it into being. Since we have already established satisfactorily that Nature works according to general laws of a universal kind (Epistles I, II) and since our study of society has shown that in that branch too the general happiness of a people allows us to judge the excellence of its forms of government (Epistle III), we can reason that happiness is something intended for everyone.

BUT, if we suppose that happiness lies in equal shares for all – and this includes qualities of mind – we would be mistaken, for one of the principles established in our look at an orderly Universe was that some are placed higher than others in certain respects: in wisdom, wealth, in power over other people:

> ORDER is Heav'n's first law; and this confest, IV, 49
> Some are, and must be, greater than the rest,
> More rich, more wise; but who infers from hence
> That such are happier, shocks all common sense.

Power and wealth do not necessarily keep company with happiness. On the contrary,

> Reason's whole pleasure, all the joys of Sense, 79
> Lie in three words, Health, Peace, and Competence.

Evil does not come from God. We must try to see evil in correct perspective, i.e. that 'partial Ill is universal Good' (113–14). Are we to expect cyclones to cease or volcanoes to stop erupting because we happen to be passing by? To the argument that virtue suffers, while vice is generally materially rewarded, Pope replies

> What then? Is the reward of Virtue bread? 150

– i.e. the good deserve not plenty but contentment. Happiness is something above earthly considerations, and luckily indestructible by things of the earth – 'the soul's calm sun-shine, and the heartfelt joy' (167). These are far above wealth and questions of social status:

> Honour and shame from no Condition rise;   192
> Act well your part, there all the honour lies.

Ancient names and noble blood cannot ennoble sots, slaves and cowards. Greatness? Does it lie with heroes or with wise men? The heroes are, many of them, lunatics; the wise men mere politicians, often villains. Fame? That is merely an imaginary life lived in the future conversation of unknown persons (237–8). In a world in which happiness is so transitory, one hour in which we can with reason think well of ourselves is worth more than years of loud praise and stupid comment (255–6). Superior mental and moral qualities? What is wisdom? It only shows us

> how little can be known;   261
> To see all others faults, and feel our own:
> Condemn'd in bus'ness or in arts to drudge
> Without a second, or without a judge:
> Truths would you teach, or save a sinking land?
> All fear, none aid you, and few understand.
> Painful pre-eminence! yourself to view
> Above life's weakness, and its comforts too.

Pope invites his readers to consider these things, and suggests that a right-thinking man will scorn them all. His only hope of certain happiness lies in virtue. In virtue only can Man taste bliss without coming close to the fall to Evil.

The close of Epistle iv shows us Pope and Bolingbroke once more, this time in another typically Augustan situation – a cultivated conversation about literature. Pope's verse, his Muse (see Chapter 1, pp. 14–21), is being schooled by Bolingbroke. And the literary terms that mark their conversation draw in moral associations as the garden images did in Epistle i:

> Teach me, like thee, in various nature wise,   377
> To fall with dignity, with temper rise;
> Form'd by thy converse, happily to steer
> From grave to gay, from lively to severe;
> Correct with spirit, eloquent with ease,
> Intent to reason, or polite to please.

They open, by implication, all pursuits and interests to moral guidance and control, summarising the main points the *Essay* has made, and leading us back full circle to a restatement of the assertion made in Epistle i, lines 21–2:

> all our Knowledge is, OURSELVES TO KNOW.   398

8

'. . . And moraliz'd his song'

In the general sweep of *An Essay on Man*, Pope's theory of the 'ruling passion' that directs the actions of each human individual could only be outlined (see Chapter 7, pp. 111–12). In his *Epistle to Viscount Cobham*, 'Of the Knowledge and Characters of Men' (1734), it is fixed upon as the only reliable guide in the difficult art of 'knowing' ourselves and assessing human character –

> Search then the Ruling Passion: There alone,   174
> The Wild are constant, and the Cunning known;
> The Fool consistent, and the False sincere;
> Priests, Princes, Women, no dissemblers here.

The informality of the epistolary mode allows Pope more variety of subject and flexibility of tone than he enjoyed in writing *An Essay on Man*. Filling in the outlines of his theory with illustrative examples, he provides as his great contemporary *exemplum* Philip, Duke of Wharton, whose disorderly career is explainable only (says the *Epistle*) by the assumption that his ruling passion was a desire for general amazement and admiration (180–209); and his small examples form a series of brief and brilliant sketches in which the rhyming couplet is put to some surprising dramatic uses, reflecting the death-bed agonies of various personages. Some of these are real, some (like Euclio) fictional:

> 'I give and I devise, (old Euclio said,   256
> And sigh'd) My lands and tenements to Ned.'
> Your money, Sir? 'My money, Sir, what all?
> Why, – if I must – (then wept) I give it Paul.'
> The Manor, Sir? – 'The Manor! hold,' he cry'd,
> 'Not that, – I cannot part with that' – and dy'd.

The insistent questions, the reluctant bequests, create not one character only but two, as the reader visualises the notary, quill-pen in hand, who writes out the will that his master's miserliness has delayed until the last possible moment. The courtier who makes his last diplomatic essay (252–5), the gourmet who feasts as he dies (234–7), the faded belle whose last thoughts are of her appearance are all equally well accommodated in Pope's flexible couplet, which not only emphasises shades of meaning but communicates atmosphere and situation:

> 'Odious! in woollen! 'twould a Saint provoke, 242
> (Were the last words that poor Narcissa spoke)
> No, let a charming Chintz, and Brussels lace
> Wrap my cold limbs, and shade my lifeless face:
> One would not, sure, be frightful when one's dead –
> And – Betty – give this Cheek a little Red.'

There is a grim, black humour in Narcissa's use of the slang word *frightful* in the context of her own approaching death that we grasp at once, although she does not. Her vocabulary, like her style of speaking, is her own; and so we are left in exquisite uncertainty whether the breaks in her voice are caused by actual shortness of breath, or by a last pathetic attempt to adopt her customary tone of affected languor.

The study of character undertaken here is matched in Pope's *Epistle to a Lady*, 'Of the Characters of Women' (1735), which examines feminine character and stresses its variety and contradictoriness. The poet's tone strikes a tactful balance between compliment and criticism that recalls the delicacy with which Miss Arabella Fermor's portrait was drawn in *The Rape of the Lock*:

> Ladies, like variegated Tulips, show, 41
> 'Tis to their Changes that their charms we owe;
> Their happy Spots the nice admirer take,
> Fine by defect, and delicately weak.

Most of Pope's pictures of contemporary Cynthias, Pastoras and Silias strike easy satirical targets: their Latin names neatly transfix the chief characteristics of Rufa, the sexy redhead, who affects to understand philosophy (21–3); of Silia, a gentle-natured girl whom a skin-blemish can, however, throw into a tantrum (29–36); of Papillia, the social butterfly whom nothing can permanently please (37–40); of the brainless, the obstinate, the compulsive takers of sedatives, the irritatingly meek (101–14). But other portraits merit more serious attention from both poet and reader, for their originals misuse or distort the gifts given them by Nature. Philomede, blessed with a discriminating taste that permits her to define expertly love's elevated nature and the delica-

cies of sexual relationships, chooses a dunce as her mate (69–86);
Flavia's spirit and intelligence turn her away from religion, and
towards a restless, self-destructive turbulence –

> Wise Wretch! with Pleasures too refin'd to please,   95
> With too much Spirit to be e'er at ease,
> With too much Quickness ever to be taught,
> With too much Thinking to have common Thought:
> Who purchase Pain with all that Joy can give,
> And die of nothing but a Rage to live.

Cloe's prudence fails to take her beyond the 'decencies' that
guide her life, into true generosity, virtue, sympathy or love (157–
80); Narcissa's selfish inconsistency renders even her occasional
well-doing worthless, and undermines everyone's respect for her
mind and morals (53–68); and Sappho's intellectual brilliance
does not excuse her slovenliness, in Pope's comparison of

> Sappho at her toilet's greasy task,   25
> With Sappho fragrant at an ev'ning Mask:
> So morning Insects that in muck begun,
> Shine, buzz, and fly-blow in the setting-sun.

In covering the day-span of an insect's short life, the four-line
portrait encapsulates the literary and personal career of Pope's
well-known contemporary, Lady Mary Wortley Montagu; once a
noted child-prodigy, her witty lampoons had later buzzed painfully about Pope's ears, and her maturer years were tarnished and
'fly-blown' with rumours of promiscuity. The images of butterfly-
like beauty, of elegance, sparkle, fragrance and grace are linked
with allusions to 'grease' and 'muck', creating a sense of fasci-
nated repulsion we will experience again in Pope's portrait of
Lord Hervey in his *Epistle to Dr Arbuthnot* (see pp. 121–34).

Taking pride of place in Pope's gallery of feminine curiosities
is his portrait of 'Atossa', based on the violent nature and restless,
litigatory public career of his contemporary, the Duchess of Buckingham. In the consistent interplay between a *tone* of adulatory
praise and a *theme* of wild inconsistency that its opening lines initiate, the portrait of Atossa –

> Scarce once herself, by turns all Womankind!   116

recalls Dryden's portrait of 'Zimri' in *Absalom and Achitophel* –

> A man so various, that he seem'd to be
> Not one, but all mankind's epitome.

The antithetical resources of successive couplets are used to demonstrate the contradictions that combine in Atossa to make her the extreme type – at its worst – of the changeableness Pope detects at the root of feminine nature (117–50).

While in the *Epistle to Viscount Cobham* Pope had demonstrated his belief that men are governed by a variety of 'ruling passions', here he asserts that women, although so changeable in themselves, are motivated chiefly only by two such driving energies: the love of pleasure, and the desire to dominate. At this point in his *Epistle*, Pope's satire gives way to an unexpected sympathy: for it is as a result of 'Man's oppression' (213) that women have learned to develop the kind of power that sustains their pleasures, and to use their beauty coldheartedly as the means to such power. Such aims, although general, are – Pope suggests – altogether too low, and their rewards too transient and negligible to be worth pursuing –

> See how the World its Veterans rewards!   243
> A Youth of frolicks, an old Age of Cards,
> Fair to no purpose, artful to no end,
> Young without Lovers, old without a Friend,
> A Fop their Passion, but their Prize a Sot,
> Alive, ridiculous, and dead, forgot!

The positives put forward in the *Epistle to a Lady* are those that Clarissa suggested to Belinda in *The Rape of the Lock*: sense, good humour, modesty and firm principles. Women, Pope suggests, should set themselves

> To raise the Thought and touch the Heart   250

and to cultivate the pleasant disposition, generosity of mind, tact and patience that illuminate private relationships, and especially that of marriage.

A closing compliment to Pope's friend, Martha Blount, playfully accusing her of possessing her own share of female contradictions, balances the portrait of Atossa by providing an example of that contradictoriness at its best –

> Reserve with Frankness, Art with Truth ally'd,   277
> Courage with Softness, Modesty with Pride,
> Fix'd Principles, with Fancy ever new;
> Shakes all together, and produces – You.

The intimate, informal tone of Pope's *Epistle to a Lady* gives the poem a 'natural' air of spontaneity from its beginning (apparently in a remark his friend had made – see lines 1–2) to its end. In his *Epistle to Dr Arbuthnot* (1735), Pope does not content himself with creating an atmosphere of friendly intimacy, but makes his poem a dramatic dialogue. Its remarkable opening –

> Shut, shut the door, good *John*! fatigu'd I said,
> Tye up the knocker, say I'm sick, I'm dead, –

plunges the reader straight into the middle of a real-life situation in which the poet, running away from the crowds of literary hacks who are dogging his steps, manages breathlessly to get into his own house, asks his servant to shut the front door and stand guard over it, and finds his old friend and physician waiting to see him – a perfect situation, in fact, to prepare the reader for the weight of self-revelation that the poem carries: the poet, being irritated and overwrought, is in a mood to speak frankly and directly, and Arbuthnot can take up the role (evidently customary with him in his relationship with Pope) of patient listener and prudent adviser.

This dramatic opening and the situation it creates falsify nothing: for Pope's intention in getting his bits and pieces together in the form of an Epistle was to 'say something of Myself' in self-defence against the libels and slanders of just such literary third-raters as the poem itself, in dramatic terms, shows him eluding. And Dr Arbuthnot's contribution to the making of the *Epistle* had been very much the same that we see him making to the 'argument' of the poem itself: a temperate, restraining influence on the poet's angry impetuosity, kindly in his view both of the poet and of his enemies, he counsels patience and caution. The *Epistle* presents us, in this way, with a concentration of the happenings of many years, and allows Pope to compose not only a defence of his own character and writings, but an unrivalled picture of those years as they affected the literary world.

> The Dog-star rages! nay 'tis past a doubt,   3
> All *Bedlam*, or *Parnassus*, is let out:
> Fire in each eye, and Papers in each hand,
> They rave, recite, and madden round the land.

The poets Pope tries to elude are seen as lunatics, residents not of Parnassus, the home of the Muses, but of Bedlam, London's hospital for the mentally deranged. The poetic 'fire' in their eyes sharpens to a lunatic gleam, and their 'reciting' becomes, by way of an alliterative link, identical with the 'raving' of mental disturbance. Paragraph 2 bears witness to their persistence, as the poet complains that he can enjoy no privacy, surrounded as he is on all sides and at all times by poets who want him to read or listen to their verses; and paragraph 3 provides examples of literary lunacy. The name of the late Poet Laureate, Laurence Eusden, inspires a witty pun –

Is there a Parson, much be-mus'd in Beer . . .   15

which suggests that *malt alcohol* and not the inspiration of the *Muses* is the cause of the *bewilderment* of *Eusden*, concentrating four levels of meaning in the one phrase 'be-mus'd in Beer'. The Parson, like the 'maudlin Poetess' and 'ryming Peer' in the next line, is either mad or vain or both, and Pope complains that he has to bear the blame for their idiocies because he is too amiable to refuse them a hearing.

In paragraph 4 this madness becomes a 'plague', and the poet applies, appropriately, to his physician for medical assistance (lines 27–30). He protests that he is liable to be murdered, either by the 'affection' of these bad writers or by their hatred. And so the poem leads, by easy stages and by the kind of logical or associative transitions that we make when moving conversationally from subject to subject (and which Pope artistically approximates in both his *Elegy to the Memory of an Unfortunate Lady* – see pp. 77–8 – and his *Essay on Man* – see pp. 100–2), to its main concern: the poet's desire to explain and explore his attitudes and actions, to 'place' his own situation, in terms of real life as well as in terms of the 'life' of literary creation.

So much is the one wrapped up in the other for this particular poet, that the *Epistle* performs several functions at the same time with great economy. And the reader may sense throughout its development that in the process of exposition and explanation there is an element of self-discovery and self-comprehension, too, at work. Like all writers everywhere and in every age, Pope understands himself better through the act of writing. As we have seen already in connection with *The Rape of the Lock*, and other poems including *The Dunciad*, the act of writing did not stop for Pope with a first draft but operated as a continuous process through draft after draft, sometimes over many years, and did not cease until the poem had been published; and not always even then. Such deliberate self-discipline involves not only artistic controls but emotional and intellectual ones, so that in a very real sense a poet can grow by the act of writing and shaping his verse. The *Epistle* contains passages of elaborate defence and lofty disquisition regarding the aim of true poetry, but it is not made up entirely of such passages. Its total achievement includes a dramatically conceived and artistically presented exercise in self-revelation: even as it sums up a lifetime of experience of many kinds, this aspect of it indicates the complex depths of the poet's character that are so perfectly mirrored in the complexities of the poem.

The variety of tones Pope adopts in the course of this poem presents some readers with difficulties (see Chapter 1, pp. 7–9): these problems tend to disappear, however, once we remember that the 'difficulties' of the poem are the 'difficulties' of the poet's personality, and stem from the range of his experiences. For there is nothing *difficult* (in the sense of being *obscure*) about his language. We are never at a loss as to the basic idea being communicated in any one line or phrase. But his language does tend toward another kind of 'difficulty', that of *complexity*. We are seldom quite certain that the meaning that does register with us is all there is in a particular phrase. The words Pope uses are Janus-faced, even (as with 'be-mus'd in', above) Protean, so that two or more meanings can arise out of apparently innocent simplicity, or be suggested by a verbal poetic device or skilful management of rhythm. And what might have appeared to us as quite straightforward at a first reading is seen to have hidden depths. And what those depths can reveal is often surprising to the reader: even, we suspect, sometimes to the poet.

In lines 33–68, Pope appears to be complaining of the attacks made upon his patience and politeness by hack writers who ask him to 'correct' their work, lend them money, help them to patronage, dine with them, get their plays on the stage and their poems in print, revise their work and share their profits . . . and so on. Under the guise of respect and friendship they seek to exploit him, and he knows it. The tone of this passage seems to be one of patient, but irritated resignation. And yet the feeling these lines express is by no means so simple. Underneath the contempt is there not also some pity for the poverty-stricken writer who must rush into print

Oblig'd by hunger and Request of friends (!)   44

who must resort to flattery, turn on a kindly critic with resentful threats, use defiance and slyness in order to make his way in the literary world? Keeping company with both these attitudes at once is another thing some readers might find hard to accept without some moral censure: Pope is writing as one who is aware of his own worth, and of his artistic superiority to those he is describing. He might profess to dislike being troubled in this manner, perhaps he does dislike it – but does he not somewhat enjoy his position as literary arbiter? Sometimes, as with many poets of lesser quality, words reveal more of a writer's soul than his art intended that they should.

What gives Pope's *Epistle* its moral power is the fact that this conscious superiority, this sense of power, is not hypocritically covered over with assumed modesty, but used for a purpose greater than that of self-praise. And here we see an instance of that paradox by which a poet writing intensely personal poetry out of subjective feelings and contemporary incidents, sometimes succeeds (because he is at one with his age) in writing poetry that is simultaneously relevant to general, even universal, concerns. He must, says Pope, like King Midas's Queen in the fable, 'speak, or burst' (lines 70–2). Telling the truth acts as a vent for suppressed, corrupting feeling. It must be done, even at the cost of personal safety:

> The truth once told, (and wherefore shou'd we lie?) 81
> The Queen of *Midas* slept, and so may I.

The transition between this passage and the next is one of Pope's best-managed: unspoken, it consists of a pause, but a pause that implies a suggestion from Arbuthnot that Pope's frankness might stem from his need of emotional relief and not from any care for the good of the world –

> You think this cruel? 83

The unspoken charge (perhaps Arbuthnot has merely raised a quizzical eyebrow!) of irresponsibility calls from Pope a brilliant exposition of the self-satisfied complacency that protects mediocrity like an armour:

> Let Peals of Laughter, *Codrus*! round thee break, 85
> Thou unconcern'd canst hear the mighty Crack.
> Pit, Box and Gall'ry in convulsions hurl'd,
> Thou stand'st unshook amidst a bursting World.

Who shames a Scribler? break one cobweb thro',
He spins the slight, self-pleasing thread anew;
Destroy his Fib, or Sophistry; in vain,
The Creature's at his dirty work again;
Thron'd in the Centre of his thin designs;
Proud of a vast Extent of flimzy lines.

The intellectual, emotional and imaginative force with which the poet's anger bursts into expression creates a whole world of rich, revolting, devastating images as the poem develops.

To illustrate the perverse insensitivity of Grub Street, Pope gives us the character of Codrus, the incompetent dramatic poet, in the style we call mock-heroic: very appropriate to the stage, on which rhetoric and heroic declamation find natural homes. Using the name of a poet who had been ridiculed by Virgil and Juvenal, Pope combines an allusion to Horace with its rendering by Addison[1] to satirise the achievement of one of his own contemporaries. 'Codrus', like one of his own theatre heroes, stands Lear-like on the stage amidst flashes of lightning and rumblings of thunder in a true heroic attitude of calm unconcern. Except that the 'Peals' are of laughter and not of lightning, the 'Crack' is an explosion of hilarity and not of thunder, and the 'convulsions' are those of playgoers straining, doubled up, rolling about in pit, box and gallery in the extremes of their amusement. And there, amidst a world 'bursting' in convulsions of contemptuous laughter stands Codrus, his calm now seen to derive from obtuseness and not from any kind of real heroism. In contrast, the 'Scribler' is seen as a spider, an image that allows Pope to build up impressions of disgust at a flimsiness and self-satisfaction that we accept as true of the subject because we feel sensuously (through his skilful manipulation of sound and association) that they are true of the insect-prototype.

When Pope leaves these general, and in some ways traditional, characters for real persons, Arbuthnot cautions him:

> No Names – be calm – learn Prudence of a Friend: 102

but by now the impulse to self-revelation and self-defence is

---

[1] Cf. Horace, *Ode* iii, 7, 8. Addison's translation:
> Should the whole frame of nature round him break,
> In ruine and confusion hurl'd,
> He, unconcern'd, would hear the mighty crack,
> And stand secure amidst a falling world.

beyond stopping, and the poem takes up matters of an intensely personal kind:

> There are, who to my Person pay their court,   115
> I cough like *Horace*, and tho' lean, am short,
> *Ammon*'s great Son one shoulder had too high,
> Such *Ovid*'s nose, and 'Sir! you have an *Eye* –'
> Go on, obliging Creatures, make me see
> All that disgrac'd my Betters, met in me:
> Say for my comfort, languishing in bed,
> 'Just so immortal *Maro* held his head:'
> And when I die, be sure you let me know
> Great *Homer* dy'd three thousand years ago.

With cynical amusement Pope calls on Arbuthnot (and the reader) to judge the lowness of the minds that will use his physical weaknesses to flatter him. The tone, dryly sardonic, is that of one who has no illusions about himself and is, as a result, beyond the reach of flattery. Intense personal feeling does not rob Pope of wit and reasoning power. The path by which a man comes to such poised self-knowledge can only be guessed at, but it is a poise to which the act of writing this very poem might have made some contribution. An extraordinarily fine critical intelligence plays over the lines, modifying, outlining, and ordering the emotional power generated there by deep feeling in much the same way that we noticed in Chapter 1, pp. 16–17, Pope's wit modifying deep personal feeling to produce the homely metaphor of the Muse of Poetry as Dr Arbuthnot's sickroom attendant (lines 131–4).

From line 125 to line 333, Pope presents the reader with a concise, concentrated autobiography, his life seen as a deliberately undertaken literary career. In the course of it he provides more pictures of those whose paths had crossed his own and in some way affected his life's work. Some of these are short, complimentary allusions to the mature, well-judging friends who encouraged his early efforts (see lines 135–42), at least one a brief, epitaph-like reference to his friend and fellow-poet, John Gay (256–60). Some are biting side-glances at inferior writers who had attacked Pope's writings or reputation: as in the lines

> Yet then did *Gildon* draw his venal quill;   151
> I wish'd the man a dinner, and sate still:

in which 'quill' combines the meanings of 'poison-pen' and the 'arrow flying in the dark' in order to hit at Gildon's lampoons written at Pope's expense. Or

> Yet then did *Dennis* rave in furious fret;   153
> I never answer'd, I was not in debt:
> If want provok'd, or madness made them print,
> I wag'd no war with *Bedlam* or the *Mint*.

recalling how Dennis's censure of *The Rape of the Lock*, left unanswered, taught Pope the art of self-control. The critics, like Bentley and Theobald, who had found fault with Pope's edition of Shakespeare and his translation of *The Iliad*, are immortalised in the *Epistle* as grubs who, having fallen into the liquid amber of great literature at the moment of its setting, are preserved to eternity by this accident –

> Each Wight who reads not, and but scans and spells,   165
> Each Word-catcher that lives on syllables,
> Ev'n such small Critics some regard may claim,
> Preserv'd in *Milton's* or in *Shakespear's* name.
> Pretty! in Amber to observe the forms
> Of hairs, or straws, or dirt, or grubs, or worms;
> The things, we know, are neither rich nor rare,
> But wonder how the Devil they got there?

Pope may be thought somewhat small-minded and vengeful here, especially in the light of his own claim, made a little earlier on, to have 'kissed the rod' of just criticism when it had been applied to his own verse (lines 157–8). But he does set out his reasons for his dismissal of academic criticism. His target is the carping critic who can't see the wood for the trees, and misses the greatness of a work in his anxiety to correct trifling points of grammar or punctuation. We recall the definition of a 'perfect Judge' in *An Essay on Criticism* as one who responds to the total harmony of a work of art, rather than to its 'peculiar Parts'. Critics such as Lewis and Theobald are the opposites of Pope's 'perfect Judge', examples of the *malignant dull*-heads whose careers (like that of Dryden's Shadwell) wage immortal war with Wit. Unable to 'read' – i.e. grasp the scope of a literary work as a whole – such commentators 'scan and spell', 'catch' words and 'live on' syllables as some frog or lizard snatches at flies and gnats. Images such as these recall the earlier reference to the 'Scribler' as a spider, and there begins to accumulate in the reader's mind a store of such associations, until at the end of the *Epistle* he too, like

Pope, sees the writers as a plague of repulsive, stinging, snapping insects and clumsy animals of the lower species who must be 'flapped' and destroyed in the interests of peace and Reason. In keeping with this line of imagery, 'wits' and 'witlings' are seen in lines 223–6 as disease-carrying insects that 'spread about the Itch of Verse and Praise' or, puppy-like,

> daggled thro' the Town,
> To fetch and carry Sing-song up and down.

The lines illustrate what 'decorum' meant for Pope in his choice of diction. He can, when there is occasion, be as grand as anyone else: we could turn, for instance, to his account of his father's life (392–405) or to his farewell to Arbuthnot at the close of the poem (406–19), both very dignified passages of a serious kind. But he can also fasten on to, and use with glee, words like 'itch' and 'daggle' in appropriate contexts: 'low' words are appropriate to the description of lower animals.

Two full-length 'characters' of contemporary literary personalities complete Pope's revolting picture of slimy animal-life, those of 'Bufo', the frog-like patron of letters, 'full-blown',

> Fed with soft Dedication all day long   233

and of 'Sporus', corrupt and lying maker of mischief, debaser of satiric poetry (which Pope regarded as a sacred tool to be used with fear and skill'[2]) to the level of lampoon, whom he presents as a combination of startling beauty with revolting dirtiness, a 'bug with gilded wings'. Bufo and Sporus are portraits that originate in recognisable contemporary personalities: Bufo being taken from the Earl of Halifax, one of those noble patrons of the Augustan age on whom writers were forced to hang, leech-like, for a living; and Sporus from Lord William Hervey, whose libellous attacks on Pope's character and family had stung him into completing and publishing the *Epistle*. Bufo's portrait is an example of scornful, elevated contempt, a satiric portrait of a man who is exploited as much as he exploits others. A receiver

> of Wits an undistinguish'd race,   237
> Who first his Judgment ask'd, and then a Place:

Bufo is a hard taskmaster, whose protégés must earn their bread

[2] See *Epilogue to the Satires* (1738), lines 212–19; also Chapter 9, pp. 139–40; Chapter I, pp. 11–12.

with devotion and humiliation; and even then it is only very rarely that he gives them a reward worth having (lines 239–44). The whole portrait is presented in tones of scornful wonder that such things should be; and, too, of thankfulness that they do since the existence of Bufo and his kind draws away some part at least of the crowds of Pope's would-be flatterers, leaving him time to devote to true genius and true friendship, like that offered him by the poet Gay (254–6).

If the portrait of Bufo is washed with scorn, that of Sporus is executed with savagery and hatred. Arbuthnot interpolates a plea that Pope should not waste his fire on a mere 'Butterfly' (305–8), thus giving Pope the cue for a full-scale treatment of Hervey as insect. He carries this out using terms that continuously parallel the attractive with the repulsive sides of a human personality until they are seen in climax to be not complementary but locked in unnatural conflict, obscene and abnormal, epitomising evil and disorder. The portrait gains added power from Pope's conviction, shared with his age, that moral virtue lay in moderation, in leaning neither 'to this side nor to that': Sporus is shown to combine extremes of beauty and corruption in himself, with nothing but 'Emptiness' at the centre of his personality. He is a nothing, a neuter, dangerous both to individuals and to society as a whole. The climax is built up gradually, every word doing its part to contrast associations of beauty and disgust:

This painted Child / of Dirt that stinks and stings	310
This Bug / with gilded wings	309
Eternal Smiles / his Emptiness betray	315
A Cherub's Face, / a Reptile all the rest	331

every imaginable poetic device being employed in the course of the passage to emphasise the points made. Pope uses *alliteration*, for instance, linking and intensifying the unpleasant associations of

*st*inks and *st*ings;

onomatopoeia, letting sound reflect and embody the sense in the hissing sibilants of

> Or at the ear of *Eve*, familiar Toad,   319
> Half Froth, half Venom, spits himself abroad

or the *poetic catalogue* in which alliteration and onomatopoeia play a subsidiary, yet intensifying part, as in

> In Puns, or Politicks, or Tales, or Lyes,   321
> Or Spite, or Smut, or Rymes, or Blasphemies.

Pope makes appropriate use of the apt, devastating *simile*, in

> Eternal Smiles his Emptiness betray,   315
> As shallow streams run dimpling all the way;

the startling *metaphor*, emphasised by the use of a triplet to exploit the idea of swinging with see-saw-like uncertainty –

> His Wit all see-saw between *that* and *this*,   323
> Now high, now low, now Master up, now Miss,
> And he himself one vile Antithesis;

or the capabilities of the *couplet* for purposes of balance, as in

> Fop at the Toilet, / Flatt'rer at the Board, /   328
> Now trips a Lady, / and now struts a Lord /;

and at last the condemnatory Biblical parallel or *allusion*, which has run as a hidden metaphor beneath every one of these comparisons, to the Serpent in the Garden of Eden. It is to this that all the reptilian and insect-images have been leading. The portrait of Sporus, with its allusion to

> Wit that can creep, and Pride that licks the dust   333

contains and climaxes them all. Ideas work back and forth throughout the portrait, relating the inconsistencies in Hervey's nature – his attractive, fashionable appearance and corrupt, devious malevolence – to a deeper psychological and physiological contradiction. Hervey's literary 'buzzing' annoys clever men and beautiful women, but being himself neither male nor female, he can neither exercise a masculine intelligence nor experience a female sensibility. The word 'enjoys' is used in a double sense – Sporus can never enjoy 'being beautiful', as a real woman might; he can never enjoy ('make love to') a beautiful woman, as a man might. Behind the sexual associations of these lines there lurks yet another, the *literary* sense in which Hervey, as a bad critic, can never be a really witty or graceful writer or appreciate true wit and grace in the writing of others. His wit is merely 'see-saw', its inconsistency revealing a sexual incompleteness –

> Now high, now low, now *Master* up, now *Miss* –

and he can even, at pleasure, change his personality and appearance –

> Now *trips* a Lady, and now *struts* a Lord,

reflecting not the virtues, but the vanities of both sexes. Prepared
for by Pope's skilful use of a rising rhythm and the literary devices
cited above, the charge that Hervey is in himself 'one vile Antithesis' carries, when it comes, the weight of more than personal
rancour. Hervey is made to seem the living negation of the 'nor-
mal' values the poem upholds, his character and actions representing abnormal deviants from the principles of Truth, Decorum and
Reason that support Augustan civilisation: the opponent of 'the
Golden Mean', since he combines in himself (and misuses) the
extremes of beauty and evil.

Such a concentrated metaphorical treatment as this of his
literary adversary by Pope goes side by side with the more traditional Drydenesque method (derived originally from Theophras-
tus) of building up a heroic character in order to break it down
with well-aimed mockery. The passage from Dryden's *Mac Flecknoe* quoted and discussed in Chapter 4 (pp. 50–2) provides a
useful illustration of this device. For the purpose of building up in
high heroic *tones* and *associations* and *images*, what he is in fact
(and at the same time) destroying with contemptuous, hard-
hitting *fact*, the rhymed couplet offers itself as an ideal tool to the
satiric poet. Its balanced rhymes afford him scope to express his
double-view of his subject, its insistence on brevity and precision
imposes on what he says an epigrammatic pointedness that can be
devastatingly effective in the speed and completeness with which
it demolishes a satiric target. Pope's portrait of 'Atticus' (193–
214) is created in this way, a tone of high praise adopted, words
such as 'Genius', 'Fame', 'Talent' and 'Art' introduced. But the
development of the passage shows how Addison's fear of competition cancels out all his virtues, so that in the end he ceases to
be a critic in the Roman tradition, his judgment swayed by fear
and flattery till he can only

> Dreading ev'n fools, by Flatterers besieg'd,   207
> And so obliging that he ne'er oblig'd;
> Like *Cato*, give his little Senate laws,
> And sit attentive to his own applause.

The poet's tone develops from praise (lines 193–6) to a delicate

complexity, poised between amusement at what is and regret at
what once was, and might have been –

> Who but must laugh, if such a man there be?   213
> Who would not weep, if *Atticus* were he!

The several portraits in this *Epistle* indicate the variety of tone
of which Pope was capable, and – especially in the Sporus
portrait – the extensive armoury of poetic devices and satiric
weapons over which he had complete control. Two more portraits remain, of Ambrose Philips and the playwright Nahum
Tate (179–90). These blend into one another, and lead up to the
great portrait of Atticus, in the same way that the spider-Scribler
portrait and Pope's sketches of buzzing wits and witlings led up
to the character of Sporus. For Philips and Tate Pope reserves a
special scorn, since their worthlessness is intensified by their complacency –

> A man's true merit 'tis not hard to find,   175
> But each man's secret standard in his mind,
> That Casting-weight Pride adds to Emptiness,
> This, who can gratify? for who can *guess*?

Philips is caricatured in a metaphor that associates his scanty
literary output with sexual impotence, and links *that* with consti-
pation –

> Just writes to make his barrenness appear,   181
> And strains from hard-bound brains eight lines a-year:

in which the assonance that links the lengthened and dragging
vowels of 'strains' and 'brains' suggests that the free, generous
flow of true artistic creativity is very far removed from this kind
of laborious and sterile effort. The portrait of Philips, with brief
references to certain other literary 'types', is made to contribute to
that of Tate, which thus contains the worst qualities of many
inferior writers, each weakness having been picked out and outlined with fine precision (183–8).

And so, from painting the portraits of his enemies in acid, Pope
passes to a self-portrait. The preliminary sketches for this have
been already executed in his sardonic self-caricature (lines 115–24)
and in a paragraph that defends his satire:

> Curst be the Verse, how well soe'er it flow,   283
> That tends to make one worthy Man my foe,

> Give Virtue scandal, Innocence a fear,
> Or from the soft-ey'd Virgin steal a tear! . . .
> A Lash like mine no honest man shall dread,
> But all such babling blockheads in his stead.

The paragraph quoted above precedes the character of Sporus. Immediately after that portrait has been drawn, his rhetoric gaining greater force and effectiveness from the implied contrast with Hervey's slyness and duplicity, Pope describes his own approach to the writing of Satire as 'manly' (367). *He* has chosen his friends and associates according to his personal ideals of virtue and worth, misled neither by wealth nor power, fashion, nor mercenary motives. *He* has never flattered, never lied (334–9). Surveying the poetry that lies now behind him, Pope goes on to make literary estimates, declaring it as being to his advantage that he did not spend too much time on verse that reflected only the workings of fancy and the imagination, but 'stoop'd' (falcon-like) to 'Truth', and moraliz'd' his song (340–1). By investing his abandonment of 'fanciful' poetry with associations of acute judgment (the falcon's eye marks its prey far off) and solidity ('moral' poetry abjures, by implication, the frothy airiness of 'fanciful' poetry, and concerns itself with real experience) Pope makes a criticism here of his own early work. It would seem that he regards the *Pastorals*, *Eloisa*, the *Elegy* and other poems of 'fancy' as inferior to *An Essay on Man*, *The Dunciad*, and the moral *Epistles*, poems informed with moral purpose. From such literary judgments (and defence, it might be noted, of certain of his works), he slips easily into the defence of his moral character.

In lines 368–81, Pope details the slander he has patiently borne without seeking vengeance, the attacks made on his morals when his writings were seen to be above criticism, the abuse that did not stop at his writings or his morals but included his deformed, sickly body, his exiled friends, and his dead father. Attributing such virtues as he might have to his parents' example, the *Epistle to Dr Arbuthnot* closes with a double farewell, a dutiful and affectionate epitaph for his father (392–405) followed by the traditional salute to the poem's dedicatee (406–19).

The *Epistle* can be regarded in many lights: as literary autobiography, as a personal testament and witty exercise in self-defence, as a survey of the contemporary literary milieu. It is all these things at once, its range of references reflecting the range of Pope's mind, his interests, and his experience, its variety of tone bearing witness to the skill with which each approach is prepared for, executed, and made to merge into the next. Above all, the *Epistle* is possibly the finest example in literature of easy and cultivated conversation. Its bantering exchanges, its flexible tone, the atmosphere it creates of intimate, yet essentially civilised communication are significant: this is the poetry most natural to Pope and to his age, poetry reflecting the social ease that characterised the coffee-house and the gentleman's club, the common interests of educated and thoughtful men. A work of Pope's maturity, the *Epistle* shows him at his best; its couplets flowing with an ease and effectiveness bestowed by a lifetime of practice, the poem presents ideas with a playful, all-sided complexity that is reflected in the words chosen to express them, and a nature that has disciplined itself to a point at which personal grudges (such as those Pope nourished against Hervey, Addison and Bentley) merge into a general and profound concern for society and its standards.

9

'A true satyrist'

'Indeed there is not in the world a greater Error, than that which Fools
are so apt to fall into, and Knaves with good reason to incourage, the
mistaking of a *Satyrist* for a *Libeller*; whereas to a *true Satyrist* nothing
is so odious as a *Libeller*, for the same reason as to a man *truly Virtuous*
nothing is so hateful as a *Hypocrite*.'

Advertisement to Pope's *Imitation of Horace*,
Book ii, Satire i

Satirists have always been open, by the nature of their writings,
to the charge that they are motivated by ill-nature, spleen and the
destructive desire to libel and lampoon rather than by any concern for society. Pope defends himself above against this charge,
just as Dryden did before him in prefaces and essays. As we have
already noted (see Chapter 7, pp. 91–2) Pope's style as a satirist is
Horatian. The 'Imitation' of a classic poet was in the eighteenth
century a genre in itself, requiring a creative, transforming talent
in the writer who attempted the difficult task of composing a
contemporary poem using the style and structure employed
originally by his famous model. Pope's *Imitations* fulfil these
requirements, but since he was convinced that even in the process of 'imitation' a true poet must reveal himself,[1] it is not surprising that a strong individuality expresses itself in his *Epistle to
Augustus* (1737).

The purpose of Horace's original poem was to praise a great
ruler; the purpose of Pope's imitation is to expose the philistinism
of King George II. The *Epistle* is necessarily, therefore, an exercise in subtlety on many levels, public, personal and literary.
After a grand opening in high panegyric, the poem's tone modu-
lates to a gentle 'reasonableness':

> We Poets are (upon a Poet's word)   358
> Of all mankind, the creatures most absurd:
> The season, when to come, and when to go,

[1] Cf. *Imitations of Horace*, Book ii, Satire i, 51–6; see also Chapter i,
p. 8.

> To sing, or cease to sing, we never know;
> And if we will recite nine hours in ten,
> You lose your patience, just like other men.

It all sounds very humble, very disarming: Pope appears to echo
sympathetically the King's impatience with men of letters, and
to agree that the list of royal priorities must rightly be very
different from that of those 'absurd' creatures, 'we Poets'. But
the deceptively honeyed manner and suavely reasonable tone
work simultaneously to *defend* the poets from the King; to reveal
their idealism and simplicity, their unworldliness (which must be
considered, in the context of the times, sheer madness), and to
shield them from the powerful philistine who seeks to brush
them out of existence as worthless and irritating nuisances –

> Yet Sir, reflect, the mischief is not great;   189
> These Madmen never hurt the Church or State:
> Sometimes the Folly benefits mankind;
> And rarely Av'rice taints the tuneful mind.
> Allow him but his Play-thing of a Pen,
> He ne'er rebels, or plots, like other men:
> Flight of Cashiers, or Mobs, he'll never mind;
> And knows no losses while the Muse is kind.
> To cheat a Friend, or Ward, he leaves to Peter;
> The good man heaps up nothing but mere metre . . .

Pope's irony defends even as it seems to attack. But as we read,
we become aware of other levels upon which the poetry functions.
The poet for whose absurdities Pope appears to apologise, is
evidently more worthy of respect than the King to whom the
plea is being made. Unlike the King, who apparently fears
rebellious and wealthy subjects will weaken his own authority
and lower his status, the 'absurd' poet is guiltless of ambition
and avarice. Pope's contempt for the King's insensitivity to literature grows silently through the length of the satire, to be vented
with enhanced force at its very end:

> And when I flatter, let my dirty leaves   415
> (Like Journals, Odes, and such forgotten things
> As Eusden, Philips, Settle, writ of Kings)
> Cloath spice, line trunks, or flutt'ring in a row,
> Befringe the rails of Bedlam and Sohoe.

Pope's indignant defence of the poet's right to compose without
interference masquerades as a deferential, self-deprecatory ad-

dress to a patron: the kind of address that his literary contemporaries had to produce in order to earn a living, and that the success of the *Iliad* had spared him from ever having to provide.

There are other senses in which these lines may be read, which reflect upon and illuminate those we have already considered. One of the these is the sense in which Pope speaks not irony, but truth: the poet does *not* affect Church or State – regrettably, since both could do with the illumination his words can provide. Another is the sense in which Pope admits the weakness and abjectness of contemporary literature: it should engage itself with public affairs, it should set its face against tyranny, but it shirks its duty, limiting itself to the private enjoyment of literary pleasure, knowing 'no losses while the Muse is kind'. A third is the sense in which all these traits are seen to result from 'madness', a disease of the mind to which poets (it is insinuated) have been traditionally prone, and of which Pope, as a sufferer of long standing, declares himself qualified to speak with authority.

In a poem written a few years later, the *Second Epistle to the Second Book of Horace Imitated* (1737), Pope develops this idea, claiming it as a reason for abandoning poetry altogether. Surely the poet who has contrived to become independent of patronage must be in need of psychiatric care if he were to go on writing of his own free will?

> But (thanks to Homer) since I live and thrive,   68
> Indebted to no Prince or Peer alive,
> Sure I should want the Care of ten *Monroes*,*
> If I would scribble, rather than repose.
>
> * Dr Monroe was physician to Bedlam Hospital
>   in Pope's time.

And yet, side by side with this disenchantment with poetry, and the often-repeated intention of abandoning it altogether, runs a ceaseless evocation of all that his art has meant for this poet:

> Years foll'wing Years, steal something ev'ry day,   72
> At last they steal us from our selves away;
> In one our Frolicks, one Amusements end,
> In one a Mistress drops, in one a Friend:
> This subtle Thief of Life, this paltry Time,
> What will it leave me, if it snatch my Rhime?
> If ev'ry Wheel of that unweary'd Mill
> That turn'd ten thousand Verses, now stands still.

The allusion to Milton's *Sonnet Written on His Twenty First Birthday* made in the words 'this subtle Thief of Life' helps to place Pope's own position: he is, in effect, Milton's descendant, meditating at the end of his career like his great predecessor at the beginning of his, on the subject of Time and Art. Helpless before Time's stealthy approach and continued pilfering, the poet dreads the possible loss of his last support, his poetic power. Losing it would involve a loss of his very 'self'.

The reference to his 'Rhime' as an 'unweary'd Mill' indicates that Pope regarded his medium and method not only as a God-given weapon, but as a man-perfected, intricate, machine-like instrument composed of interlocking and smoothly-running parts, capable of producing not only quantity (it produces 'ten thousand Verses' with an ease that is poetically underlined by the casualness of the phrase) but quality: for 'turn'd' in line 79 does not only mean 'turned out' in the sense that a chocolate mill turns cocoa beans out in the form of powder, but 'perfected', 'finished', smoothly 'crafted' as a mass of clay is 'turned' by a potter's wheel or a block of wood by a carpenter's lathe, into a shapely and functional object. Pope's 'unweary'd Mill' has many 'wheels' turning in unison, not just one: for Pope the heroic couplet was a delicate, sophisticated instrument, capable of many and varied uses in the skilled hands of a master-craftsman, capable of refining image, sound and sense to new, unexpected brilliance. So much has 'Rhime' become the poet's essential self, the mirror of varied moods and a multiplicity of interests, that he cannot contemplate unmoved a life in which increasing age or ill health might deprive him of the ability to compose.

In easy, conversational verse, Pope begins to talk of giving up the writing of poetry before his skills grow blunt, and turning to philosophy:

> Well, on the whole, *plain* Prose must be my fate: 198
> Wisdom (curse on it) will come soon or late.
> There is a time when Poets will grow dull:
> I'll e'en leave Verses to the Boys at school:
> To Rules of Poetry no more confin'd,
> I learn to smooth and harmonize my Mind,
> Teach ev'ry Thought within its bounds to roll,
> And keep the equal Measure of the Soul.

Philosophy (on the advice of Lord Bolingbroke, who became for

Pope in these years the voice of Reason[2]) is now to take the place poetry has hitherto occupied in his life. This stance was, however, rudely shaken in the same year of 1737, when Pope's philosophical poem written under Bolingbroke's influence, *An Essay on Man* (see Chapter 7, pp. 100–93), was attacked by Crousaz, Professor of Mathematics and Philosophy at Lausanne. Pope did not attempt a reply[3] but he was taught by the incident that philosophy was not his natural sphere. Returning to poetry of a satiric kind, Pope published his brilliant *Epilogue to the Satires* in 1738.

In this poem, the Muse of Poetry reappears to bless the poet's use of the satiric mode. 'Diadem'd, with Rays divine', blazing with virtuous light, using her powers to protect the good from oblivion, the Muse's influence

> guards the Poet, sanctifies the line, 246
> And makes Immortal, Verse as mean as mine

as long, says Pope, as that verse is dedicated to the same purpose. In a passage that looks back to the fervour of his *Epistle to Dr Arbuthnot*, Pope presents his view of satiric poetry and of his own contribution to it:

> *Fr.* You're strangely proud.
>   *P.* So proud, I am no Slave: 205
> So impudent, I own myself no Knave:
> So odd, my Country's Ruin makes me grave.
> Yes, I am proud; I must be proud to see
> Men not afraid of God, afraid of me:
> Safe from the Bar, the Pulpit, and the Throne,
> Yet touch'd and sham'd by *Ridicule* alone.
>   O sacred Weapon; left for Truth's defence,
> Sole Dread of Folly, Vice, and Insolence!
> To all but Heav'n-directed hands deny'd,
> The Muse may give thee, but the Gods must guide.
> Rev'rent I touch thee! but with honest zeal;
> To rowze the Watchmen of the Publick Weal,
> To Virtue's Work provoke the tardy Hall,
> And goad the Prelate slumb'ring in his Stall.

[2] See *Imitations of Horace*, Book I, Epistle I (1738), lines 11–16. Here verse is likened by Pope to 'Love, and ev'ry Toy,/The rhymes and rattles of the Man or Boy' (17–18).

[3] A defence of *An Essay on Man* was undertaken by William Warburton, a priest and theologian who was Chaplain to Frederick, Prince of Wales. Pope's gratitude may be measured by the fact that he made Warburton his literary executor, left him half his library and also the profits of his posthumous works.

Poetry cloaks the poet in a 'strange' mantle of pride, becoming the sacred weapon he wields in a personal war on Folly, Vice, Insolence, and the corruption in public life that is the cause of his 'Country's Ruin'. In having been permitted to wield it effectively, Pope claims that he has been 'Heav'n-directed'. These are high claims: and we recall the distinction he makes in his Advertisement to Book II, Satire I of *Horace Imitated* (see p. 135) between satirist and libeller, the man of virtue and the hypocrite. His brief sojourn in philosophical 'harmonizing' has not robbed his wit of its agility: within a line and a half of this elevated passage, the satiric rapier that 'touch'd' the corrupt public figure in lines 210–11 becomes a 'goad' that will prod a reluctant State and sleepy Church into action. The double meaning (of cattle-stall and church-pew) pressed into the word 'Stall' defines for us exactly the ox-like stupidity, the heavy lumbering indifference Pope objects to in the clergy, guardians of the nation's moral health.

Pope's ability to transcend in satire the limited heights of lampoon and personal attack becomes especially clear when we examine *The Dunciad*, and compare its versions of 1728 and 1742–3. The compass of the poem we considered in Chapter 6 (pp. 81–9) widens in the later version as Pope turns from the theme of Dulness in literature to that of Dulness as the source of general moral and intellectual enervation. The poem embraces a whole environment, and does not limit itself to exploring literary concerns only, although Books III and IV of the final version build on passages first written for the version of 1728 and first published as its third Book. In taking a wide, darkly pessimistic survey of the eighteenth-century milieu, *The Dunciad* ranges from farce, burlesque and indecency to sensuous aural and verbal effects and mock-elevation of a Drydenesque grandeur, depicting a world in which true learning and the achievements of the mind have been replaced by enthusiasm and ignorance, where squalid Grub Street standards substitute for the homogeneity of the coffee-house and the salon, and where Satire itself fails: not because society has no further need of its corrective, healing powers, but because the moral values that supported society have themselves fallen into decay.

The development of *The Dunciad* in range and scope from the version of 1728 to that of 1743 reveals itself in the rewriting of key passages. We could look, for example, at the *Variorum* (1728) lines 109–20, with its portrait of Lewis Theobald, the favourite son of the Goddess of Dulness:

> She ey'd the Bard, where supperless he sate,   109
> And pin'd, unconscious of his rising fate;
> Studious he sate, with all his books around,
> Sinking from thought to thought, a vast profound!
> Plung'd for his sense, but found no bottom there;
> Then writ, and flounder'd on, in mere despair.
> He roll'd his eyes that witness'd huge dismay,
> Where yet unpawn'd, much learned lumber lay,
> Volumes, whose size the space exactly fill'd;
> Or which fond authors were so good to gild;
> Or where, by sculpture made for ever known,
> The page admires new beauties, not its own.

Theobald's supperless condition, caused by the poverty of his writing and publishing, is ironically explained: 'the true Critic' prefers the 'diet of the mind' to the over-indulgence 'of the body'. The archaic word 'sate' dresses Theobald in incongruous state as a legendary hero, which the rising rhythm and tone of praiseful panegyric supports, even as the text (which shows him *sinking* and *floundering* without dignity) cuts it down to its proper size. The final six lines dwell on the 'learned lumber' that makes up Theobald's library, suggesting that he chooses his books for reasons other than their literary value.

If we compare this portrait with Pope's rewriting of it in the 1743 version to suit the character of his new hero, the playwright and actor Colley Cibber, we will notice a series of significant alterations:

> Swearing and supperless the Hero sate,   115
> Blasphem'd his Gods, the Dice, and damn'd his Fate.
> Then gnaw'd his pen, then dash'd it on the ground,
> Sinking from thought to thought, a vast profound!
> Plung'd for his sense, but found no bottom there,
> Yet wrote and flounder'd on, in mere despair.
> Round him much Embryo, much Abortion lay,
> Much future Ode, and abdicated Play;
> Nonsense precipitate, like running Lead,
> That slip'd thro' Cracks and Zig-zags of the Head;
> All that on Folly Frenzy could beget,
> Fruits of dull Heat, and Sooterkins of Wit.

> Next, o'er his Books his eyes began to roll,
> In pleasing memory of all he stole,
> How here he sipp'd, how there he plunder'd snug
> And suck'd all o'er, like an industrious Bug.
> Here lay poor Fletcher's half-eat scenes, and here
> The Frippery of crucify'd Moliere;
> There hapless Shakespear, yet of Tibbald sore,
> Wish'd he had blotted for himself before . . .

A reputation for pedestrianism and plagiarism provides the cue
for a view of the writer as a blood-sucking parasite. The best lines
of the 1728 version have been retained (112–14, for example) but
gain added power in their new context. The mock-heroic of the
Theobald portrait is heightened in Pope's implicit comparison of
Homer's classic heroes with his own 'lively Dunce' sulking,
Achilles-like, in his library. The contrast between the monumental
disasters that befall Homer's warriors and Cibber's ludicrous
situation (brought on by gambling losses) is established through
the tension generated in the poem as Pope's elevated tone works
against the triviality of his subject. The opening lines of the
portrait thus exemplify in a small way the tendency of Cibber
and his like to magnify the trivial and insignificant.

This contrast is maintained in the next lines, as Cibber's literary
clumsiness is implicitly and incongruously linked with the Muse-
directed divine flights of the true poet. The action of 'gnawing
his pen', then 'dashing it on the ground' would have been appropriate to a dramatic hero – a Brutus, perhaps, or a Coriolanus –
in desperate straits. Here the drama is undermined by the suggestion that Cibber's heroics belong in the same category as a
child's tantrums or the blame a bad workman reserves for his
tools. Next, the 'learned lumber' of the 1728 version undergoes a
profound change: from indicating Theobald's intellectual limitations in a passage subsidiary to the main portrait, it becomes the
real centre of the new portrait of Cibber –

> Round him much Embryo, much Abortion lay . . .

The writings of Pope's new hero are described in terms of arrested
or miscarried fertility: 'embryo' and 'abortion' surround Cibber
in the form of half-written manuscripts, half-hopes for future
poems, notes for abandoned plays. These monsters are seen as the
misshapen children of Cibber's ruling spirits, Folly and Frenzy.
(A union of Reason with Imagination or Fancy would have

produced a healthy progeny, but Cibber knows nothing of *them*.)
His head filled with leaden 'Nonsense', his only wit is the mouse-
like 'Sooterkin' bred in his brain by its own 'dull Heat', as it
was commonly thought to be bred in their bodies by Dutchwomen
through their constant use of hot stoves in winter. The introduction at this point of such an irreverent popular allusion removes the last trace of heroism from the portrait of Cibber, and
subtly reinforces the impressions of physical debility already
established by the words 'embryo' and 'abortion', initiating a
sense of repulsion in the reader that is soon to find its justification
in

> Next, o'er his Books his eyes began to roll,
> In pleasing memory of all he stole,
> *How here he sipp'd, how there he plunder'd snug*
> *And suck'd all o'er, like an industrious Bug.*

Seen in his true relation to great literature, Cibber is nothing
more than a disgusting and parasitic insect, his plagiarism of the
great dramatists a furtive 'sipping', 'sucking', and 'stealing' of
human blood. And yet Pope's description includes a sensuousness,
a light, butterfly-like gaiety that recall Pope's portraits of Lord
Hervey and Lady Mary Wortley Montagu in the *Epistles*
written to Dr Arbuthnot and to Miss Martha Blount (pp. 119,
129–30). It is through the key-word 'sucked' that feeling modu-
lates to convey his sense of the bug's revolting 'industry'. Cibber
and his habits revolt us, and by inducing such revulsion in his
reader Pope indicates how bad writing and criticism can damage
and ultimately destroy a cultural and moral fabric: Cibber's helpless, mutilated victims are the great works of Fletcher, Shakespeare
and Molière. The deliberately inelegant allusions to 'Sooterkin'
and 'Bug' energise, without destroying, the poise of Pope's mock-
heroic tone; and the flow of ridicule continues as Cibber gloats
over the plagiarisms that comically parallel the achievements of
the Greek heroes, and soliloquises in praise of Dulness (i, 173–6).

The portrait of Cibber, with its magnificent insect-image,
builds, therefore, on the 1728 portrait of Theobald, but draws its
greatest effects from the numerous allusions to grubs and lower
animals in that version (see Chapter 6, pp. 85–6). These images
reach a climactic immensity in Book iv of the final *Dunciad*,
with its glimpses of hack writers swarming around their Goddess
as

> orb in orb, conglob'd are seen IV, 79
> The buzzing Bees about their dusky Queen

or crowding

> thick as Locusts black'ning all the ground. IV, 397

Pope's allusions to asses, puppies and dab-chicks in the 1728 version experience a comparable expansion, and culminate in his magnificent portrait of the scholar Bentley, seen first as a clumsy whale in Cambridge streams; once he was

> tempestuous wont to sport IV, 201
> In troubled waters, but now sleeps in Port

and wakes from a comfortable after-dinner nap to march in the van of Dulness's votaries, proclaiming himself her

> mighty Scholiast, whose unweary'd pains IV, 211
> Made Horace dull, and humbled Milton's strains.
> Turn what they will to Verse, their toil is vain,
> Critics like me shall make it Prose again.

Lively, flowing apparently with the greatest possible ease, Pope's verse seems to be controlled by a hidden power that can bend anything to poetic purposes. Invective is directed against all the follies of the age, the politicians and patrons, scientists and people of fashion, bad writers and sycophants whose activities 'prop the Throne' of Dulness. Pope's sensuous description of the slumber brought on by the reading of dull poets in the 1728 *Variorum* –

> Soft, creeping, words on words, the sense compose, II, 357
> At ev'ry line they stretch, they yawn, they doze.
> As to soft gales top-heavy pines bow low
> Their heads, and lift them as they cease to blow,
> Thus oft they rear, and oft the head decline,
> As breathe, or pause, by fits, the airs divine:
> And now to this side, now to that, they nod,
> As verse, or prose, infuse the drowzy God

reappears without alteration as lines 389–96 of Book II in the final *Dunciad*, but is expanded unforgettably in Book IV as the Goddess's heroic yawn initiates a creeping paralysis of will and effort that spreads throughout the land:

> More had she spoke, but yawn'd – All Nature nods: IV, 605
> What Mortal can resist the Yawn of Gods?
> Churches and Chapels instantly it reach'd;
> (St. James's first, for leaden Gilbert preach'd)

Then catch'd the Schools; the Hall scarce kept awake;
The Convocation gap'd, but could not speak:
Lost was the Nation's Sense, nor could be found,
While the long solemn Unison went round:
Wide, and more wide, it spread o'er all the realm;
Ev'n Palinurus nodded at the Helm:
The Vapour mild o'er each Committee crept;
Unfinish'd Treaties in each Office slept;
And Chiefless Armies doz'd out the Campaign;
And Navies yawn'd for Orders on the Main.

The skill that made verse enact the swaying of trees in 'soft gales'
in lines 359–60 of the *Variorum* sets itself above to recreate the
infectious influence of a yawn. As a general drowsiness sweeps
Britain, it is noticeable (we cannot miss the ironic, alliterative
glance at 'Churches' and 'Chapels') that some parts of society
are more susceptible to this sleeping sickness than others. The
'unfinish'd Treaties' that 'sleep' in government 'offices' recall the
'Chaos' described in Book I,

> Where nameless Somethings in their causes sleep.   I, 56

And so the poem moves into a vision of gathering darkness, as
civilisation spins backwards into original chaos, lights that were
still glowing in Book I go out one by one, and Grub Street prepares to take over the world:

> In vain, in vain, – the all-composing Hour   IV, 627
> Resistless falls: The Muse obeys the Pow'r.
> She comes! she comes! the sable Throne behold
> Of *Night* Primaeval, and of *Chaos* old!
> Before her, *Fancy's* gilded clouds decay,
> And all its varying Rain-bows die away.
> *Wit* shoots in vain its momentary fires,
> The meteor drops, and in a flash expires.
> As one by one, at dread Medea's strain,
> The sick'ning stars fade off th'ethereal plain;
> As Argus' eyes by Hermes' wand opprest,
> Clos'd one by one to everlasting rest;
> Thus at her felt approach, and secret might,
> *Art* after *Art* goes out, and all is Night.

Although conceived as a confrontation between the powers of
light and darkness, there is no heroic conflict here; caught in the
divine languor of Dulness, even Pope's Muse can do nothing and
every familiar moral, artistic and intellectual beacon fades in-
gloriously away as the Goddess draws near:

> See skulking Truth to her old Cavern fled,   641
> Mountains of Casuistry heap'd o'er her head!
> *Philosophy*, that lean'd on Heav'n before,
> Shrinks to her second cause, and is no more.
> *Physic* of *Metaphysic* begs defence,
> And *Metaphysic* calls for aid on *Sense*!
> See *Mystery* to *Mathematics* fly!
> In vain! they gaze, turn giddy, rave, and die.
> *Religion*, blushing veils her sacred fires,
> And unawares *Morality* expires.

The note of tragic inevitability that sounds throughout Pope's 'celebration' of the triumph of all that he loathes arises from his awareness that the forces of light are in total disarray. Betraying weakness and fear, the heroic positives of old – Truth, Morality, Religion and the arts – offers no defence, their only actions the negative ones of 'skulking', 'shrinking', 'expiring' and 'blushing'. The passage blends the Greek and Christian myths of creation in order to draw from the tragedy of their reversal something of the dignity and resonance of these great originals:

> Nor *public* Flame, nor *private*, dares to shine;   651
> Nor *human* Spark is left, nor Glimpse *divine*!
> Lo! thy dread Empire, CHAOS! is restor'd;
> Light dies before thy uncreating word:
> Thy hand, great Anarch! lets the curtain fall;
> And Universal Darkness buries All.

The magnificent closing couplets flood Pope's witty, learned and allusive description with intense feeling. Where God had said, 'Let there be light' and initiated His creation, the word of Chaos is 'uncreating', and leans toward death and oblivion. In these final scenes of cosmic, undefended destruction, we perceive a tension between tone and subject very different from the easy, satiric banter of *The Rape of the Lock*. Despite the Rabelaisian scenes that have preceded it, the surrealistic chaos in which the poem ends strikes us as tragic, irreversible, and beyond the power of Satire to arrest.

There has been implicit in all Pope's poetry up to this point a comprehensive and balanced attitude to life based on the notion of an ordered universe. *An Essay on Man* pithily presented the essence of moral and philosophical thinking in its time, *An Essay on Criticism* restated inherited critical maxims, and breathed new life into traditional concepts and methods by relating them to contemporary poetical and critical practice. *The Rape of the Lock* and the *Satires* and *Moral Epistles* surveyed Pope's immediate world, pointing out ways to reform what was defective and sustain what was not. But as we read the last book of *The Dunciad*, we become aware that the values that support the body of his poetry do not have much longer to live. Written in the year before his death, it tells a story of disrupted standards and disappointed ideals, and describes a disordered, irreparably damaged universe. The code of the mock-heroic genre within which he works keeps the tone of the poem in control throughout, but we are aware as we come to the end of it that the great period of Augustan civilisation is drawing, with Pope's life and his poetry, to a close. It may well have been that in writing *The Dunciad* he found a way of coming to terms – however temporarily – with disillusionment and disaster, maintaining in it the artistic balance between Reason and Passion that was the only kind of order still in his power to create.

Index of passages quoted

DATE DUE

WITHDRAWN